THE LAND OF THE ETRUSCANS

from Prehistory to the Middle Ages

edited by Salvatore Settis

Texts by Marisa Bonamici, Riccardo Francovich,
Renata Grifoni Cremonesi, Andreina Ricci
and Leonardo Rombai

Drawings by Giovanni Caselli

SCALA

The publisher wishes to dedicate this book to the memory of Ferruccio Marchi, master designer, art publisher and Florentine gentleman.

CONTENTS

In order to enable the reader immediately to distinguish between the different historical periods dealt with in each of the nine geographical areas examined, the first part of every chapter (dealing with prehistory) has been set in *italics*, the second part (Etruscan and Roman period) is in roman, and the third (Early Middle Ages) is in a smaller typeface.

The texts are by the following authors:
Renata Grifoni Cremonesi – Prehistory
Marisa Bonamici – Etruscan period
Andreina Ricci – Roman period
Riccardo Francovich – Early Middle Ages

Cover: stone statue of Apollo from the sanctuary of Scasato at Falerii, inspired by a statue of Alexander the Great by the Greek sculptor Lysippus (late 4th century B.C.). Rome, Villa Giulia.

Title page: the tomb known as "Pythagoras's lair" at Cortona (2nd century B.C.).

Back cover: a tomb in the necropolis of Norchia (4th-3rd century B.C.).

1. Tarquinia, end wall of the "Tomba degli Auguri" (540-520 B.C.). On either side of the doorway, which symbolized the world of the dead, two figures greet the onlooker.

Editing: Daniele Casalino
Layout: Fried Rosenstock
Drawings: Giovanni Caselli
Maps: Ilaria Casalino
Produced by SCALA
Photographs: SCALA (M. Falsini, N. Grifoni, M. Sarri) with the exception of: nn. *53* (F. Papafava); *85, 86, 115* (Pubbliaerfoto, Milan); *116* (Archaeological Museum, Grosseto); p. 89/II, III, IV (R. Francovich)
Printed in Italy by Kina Italia, Milano 1997

1

PREFACE

The land of the Etruscans is not simply the stage on which their remarkable history unfolded. It played an important role in the long line of events that began well before the formation of the Etruscan nation and continued beyond its slow assimilation within the civilization of Rome.

The territory between the Tiber and the Arno, both because of its variety of landscape and potential resources (from its vast forests to its mineral reserves) and because of the balance between inland and coast (ideal for maritime trade), offers us the essential elements for an understanding of its history. And, conversely, it is the work of the historians and archaeologists that allows us to reconstruct the characteristics of the natural environment in different periods. Hilltop villages and the development of urban communities; regulation of watercourses and agrarian organization of the land; development of communication routes, by river or on land (up to the Roman roads); manufacturing, agricultural and trading activities; mechanisms of cultural and social differentiation: in all these spheres man and the land are the protagonists. And it is not a casual collection of events, but a complex historical development, from which spring the roots of our present.

Following a circular geographic route, from Veii northwards to Fiesole and Pisa, and then south again to Tarquinia and Caere, this book attempts to illustrate the history of each area. Our sources are mostly archaeological finds, rather than written documents. Our historical survey goes beyond the Etruscan and Roman periods to the early Middle Ages, but it is not our intention to prove the existence of a continuity that too many facts could easily refute. We intend merely to illustrate the essential elements of an exemplary case of close interaction between man and the land he lives on.

Salvatore Settis

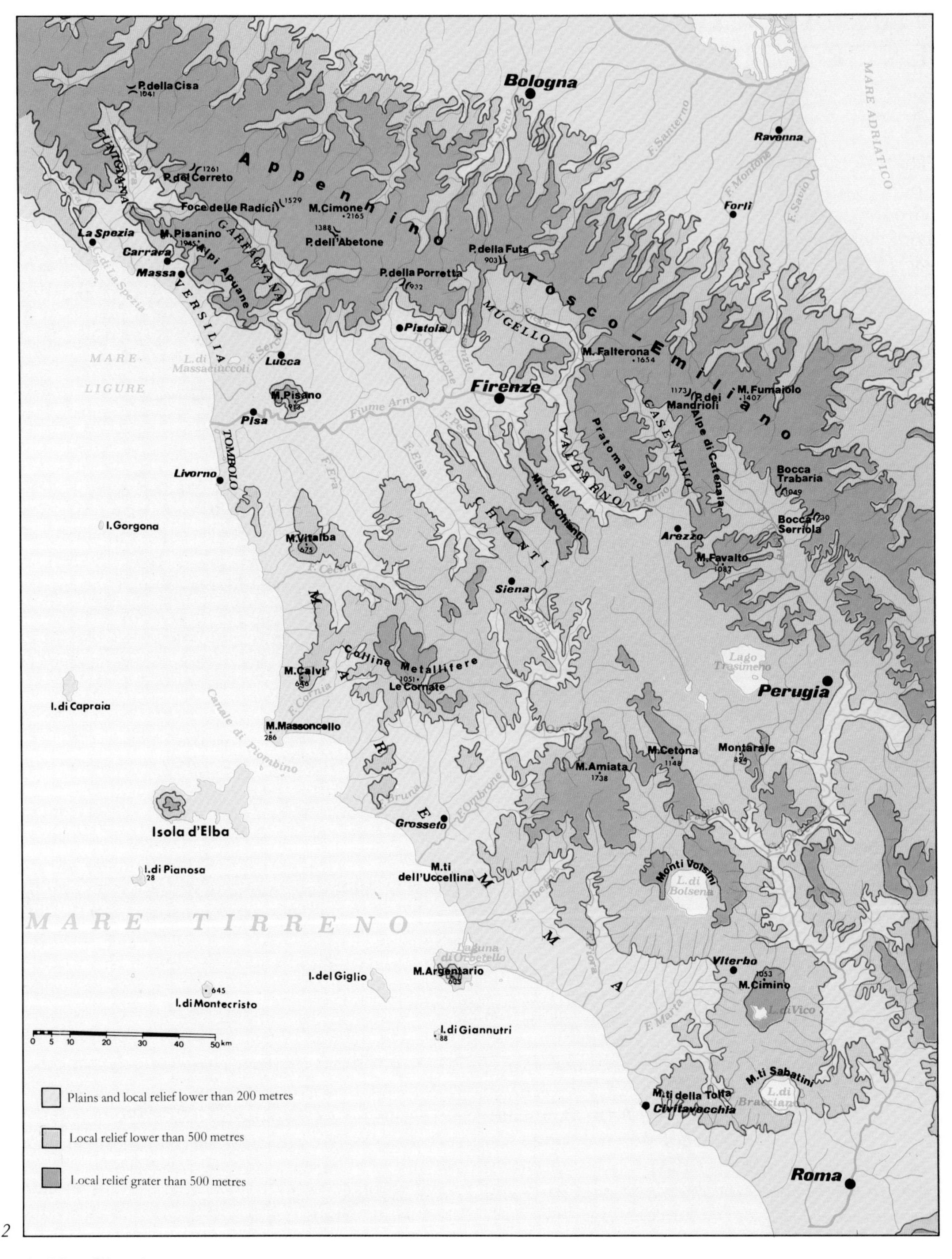

2

2. *Map of Etruria.*

THE NATURAL ENVIRONMENT

by Leonardo Rombai

Thanks to both historical and archaeological sources, we are able to reconstruct the major environmental features of Etruria, as well as the complex role played by the natural habitat (geological structure and development of the soil, climate, inland watercourses and coastline, flora).

The area between the Tiber and the Arno—and also the stretch of land further north, as far as the River Magra and the Appennines, annexed by Augustus to the 7th Region—was basically not very different at the time of the Etruscans from what it is like now. Some aspects of the landscape, however, must have been quite different, although these changes are not the work of nature, but of man, who over the past two and a half thousand years (albeit somewhat discontinuously) has caused the destruction of a great deal of the spontaneous flora and the alteration of its composition. Man has changed the course of rivers and dried the plains, he has built towns, villages and roads.

By the first millennium B.C., the inland plains, in the mountainous areas around the Appennines, were no longer marshy, and the plains near the coast had been created by the filling in of the gulfs, while all volcanoes in Tuscany and Latium had already been extinct for thousands of years. Even the structure of the mountains (shapes, position, altitude and slope) was almost exactly the same as it is today; the earth's surface has simply been lowered—the result of erosion—by one or two metres. The only topographical element that differs in any considerable way is the coastline near flat areas, where the rivers, with their silt, have slowly filled in all the marshy areas. As early as the 7th-6th centuries B.C. the dunes along the coast had already formed into continuous sandbars, creating a barrier isolating the inland marshy lakes from the sea. In other words the coastline consisted in crescent-shaped inlets alternating with promontories—as is, for the most part, still the case—but did not have the pronounced jutting areas around the deltas of the Tiber, the Arno and the Ombrone. The mouths of these rivers were actually recessed by five kilometres in the case of the first two, and by two in the case of the Ombrone.

Large expanses of marshland also filled some of the lower-lying inland plains, for the rivers fre-

3

3. The mountainous beech wood on Mount Amiata.

quently flooded. The rivers' courses were characterized by curves and bends, with many ramifications; all the beds were very wide and obviously without any artificial banks. The River *Clanis* flowed towards the Tiber directly from Arezzo, the Serchio (*Auser*) ran south of Lucca and one branch emptied into the Lake of Bientina, the other into the Arno at Pisa. The Ombrone originally flowed into Lake Prile until it managed, at the beginning of the Christian era, to change its course sufficiently to empty directly into the sea. Yet, basically, the course of the rivers was not too different from that of today.

Before the development of the Etruscan society and economy, the flora of the region consisted primarily in woods. The changes in climate which occurred after the pre-historical eras did not modify the characteristics of the natural flora established after the last ice age: starting from the coastline and moving towards the highest peaks of the Appennines, there were a succession of fundamental botanical groupings, more or less the same as today. These began with the Mediterranean evergreen shrub (without, however, the umbrella pine, which was only introduced by the Romans); there then followed the Submediterranean dry wood, consisting primarily in pubescent oak, and the Submountainous Turkey oak wood, both of them without chestnut-trees which, although indigenous, spread after the Middle Ages as cultivated trees; and finally the Mountainous beech wood, also including many conifers such as the silver fir and the Norway spruce.

At that time there must also have been large

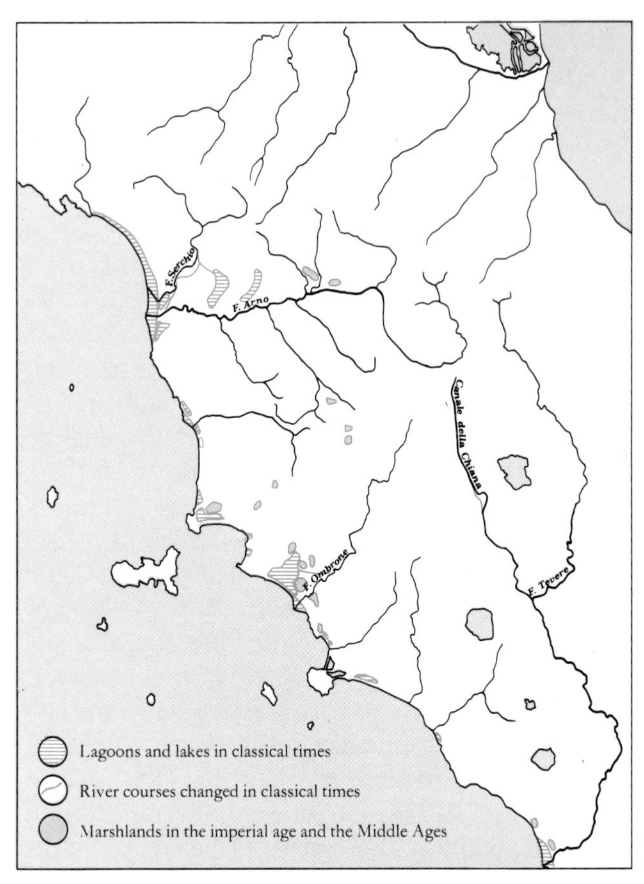

4. The mountainous silver fir wood on Mount Amiata; in the distance the clay hills of Radicofani.

5. Hydrographic map of Etruria.

stretches of plain-growing forest, made up of alder, elm, common oak, poplar, willow and ash which—together with the hydrophyte herbaceous and shrubby vegetation typical of damp areas—developed throughout the marshy lands and around the lagoons and wherever the surface was covered with water. Today there are only small areas of it left at San Rossore near Pisa.

The development and expansion of the Etruscan civilization caused a gradual but profound transformation of the environment, particularly in terms of water courses and flora. The Etruscans deserve their fame as expert regulators of water courses. They radically changed the appearance of the marshy plains and lagoons, not by actual drainage, but probably through a widespread series of works increasing the natural (and, in some cases, artificial) drainage of the water, in order to make the agricultural land permanently cultivable and the level of the lakes uniform, thus making fishing and navigation possible. At the same time, on the higher plains and on the coastal and inland hills, they began to exploit the resources of the forests, using the wood to build ships and houses and as fuel for the metal industry. The clearings were used as cultivable land and pasture.

Under the Etruscans, the increased number of human settlements, the drainage systems and the introduction of the plough allowed for the widescale cultivation of grain and textile fibres, of vines and fruit trees. This form of agriculture changed the appearance of the landscape, creating the geometric pattern of "closed fields" (with the vines, tied high up to their supporting trees, in straight rows marking the borders of the square fields). All the areas around the settlements in south ern Etruria began to have this regular appearance. The only exception was the stretch north of the Arno—a natural border between the Etruscans and the Ligurians—which was only won over to this kind of agricultural colonization in the 2nd century B.C. when the consular roads, the Cassia and the Aurelia, were extended to Luni.

The Romans reorganized and further developed this system of regular square plots in the plains with mixed cultivation, at the expense of the wood and pasture land. They introduced the cultivation of the olive and of the cypress, which flourished at least until the end of the late republican age. Later, the transition from small, single-family farm units to the large landed estates based on slave labour led to the degradation and regression of the agricultural areas—especially at the time of the later Roman Empire—with an increase

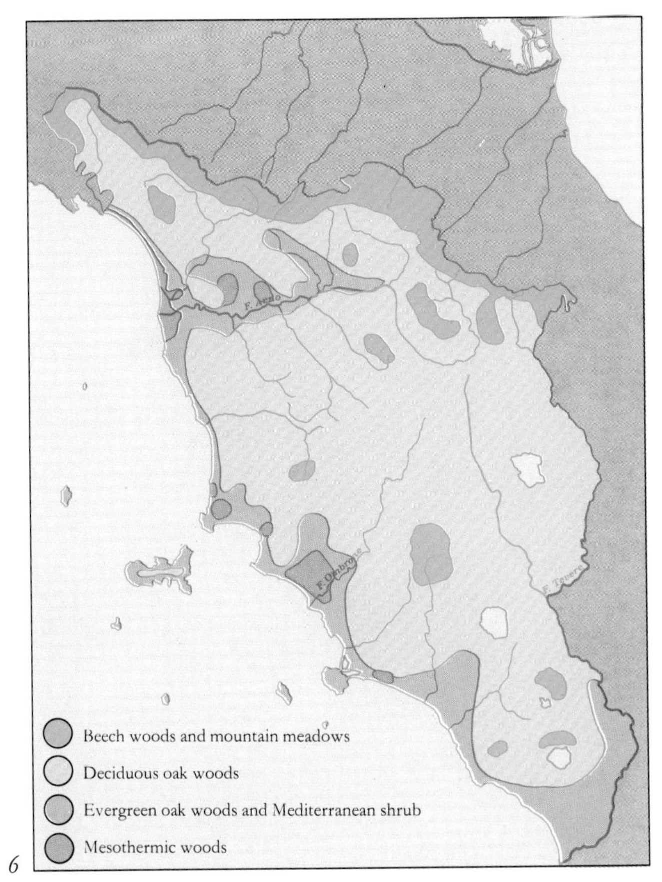

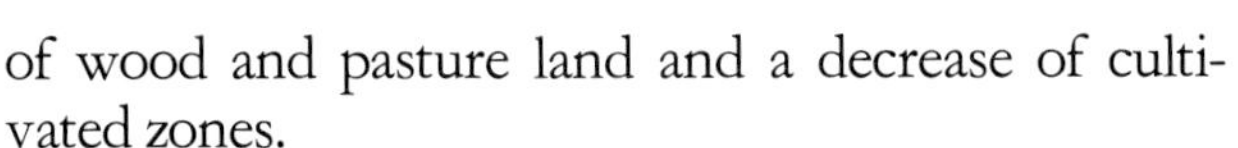

6

7

6. *Map of the spontaneous vegetation in Etruria.*

7. *The river Fiora, which marks the northern border of volcanic Etruria.*

of wood and pasture land and a decrease of cultivated zones.

In other words, the natural environment offered huge possibilities to a culturally and technologically developed society. Firstly, the conformation of the land and the composition of the soil were favourable to agriculture, for there were many fertile stretches (the volcanic soil on the plateaux of Tuscany and Latium and the irrigation provided by the flooding of rivers on the plains) which the Etruscans cultivated with very advanced agricultural techniques. The mineral resources in the central and western part of the region—the so-called "mineral Etruria"—are also connected with the geological formation: the top soil, consisting in clay and calcareous deposits and sandstone, allowed easy access to the older formations below, rich in copper, tin, lead containing silver, iron, cinnabar, ochre and so on.

Almost all the towns and the minor agricultural centres were built on top of hills, the so-called "Etruscan position." This is undoubtedly connected with the geological characteristics of the region: the Etruscans grasped the exceptional defensive advantages offered by the narrow tufa plateaux, from which they could keep watch over the valleys, the rivers, the fords, the coastal ports and the towns on the hillsides. This choice—which also offered more favourable climatic conditions—was determined by the Etruscan political set-up and not, as some would have it, by the fact that the plains were uninhabitable because of flooding or malaria. And in fact, when the region was unified under the Romans, settlements sprang up throughout the plains.

The natural resources were copious. The immense forests produced wood for building and for fuel, which was also used in the mining industry. The manufacturing industry prospered thanks to the ample water supplies, to the easy access to mineral deposits and to ports for export. At the mouths of the major rivers, as well as in the inlets between the promontories, there were safe harbours for trading vessels; the river valleys were important communication routes with the interior. Etruria's very position, *umbilicus Italiae*, was extraordinarily favourable.

The coastal lagoons, like the Prile, offered inexhaustible reserves of fish and wildlife as well as shelter for boats. The hygienic condition of the coast and of the Tiber and Chiana valleys must have been fairly good, since several settlements sprang up in these areas which later were to be so deadly. Malaria, if there was any at all, certainly

8

9

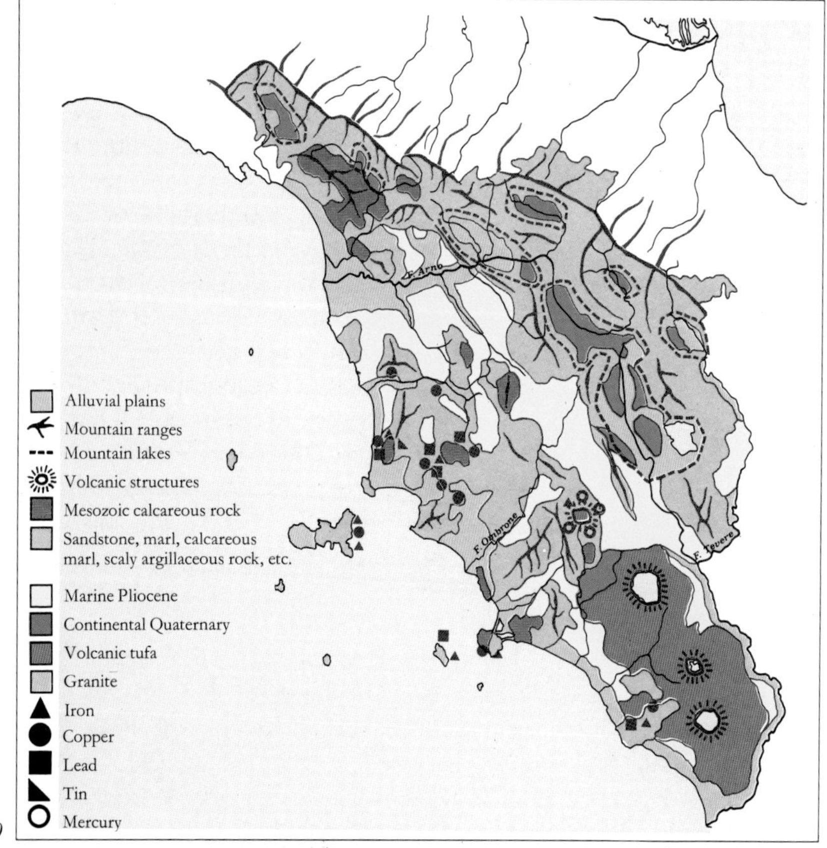

8. A vineyard at Sorano, growing on the tufa terraces.

9. Geomorphological and mineral map of Etruria.

10. Lake Accesa, which lies in the middle of a large mineral basin exploited during classical times.

did not constitute a serious menace, for the population led a very active and productive life. It was not until the 3rd-5th centuries A.D. that malaria reached the height of its destructive power.

During the period of the Roman Empire, however, the creation of large landed estates and the decline of productive activities and trade—since Etruria was no longer on the major communication routes between Rome and the Po valley—caused the economic decline of the cities. The population of the cities decreased and many coastal towns were abandoned completely; new "castles" were built on the hilltops in the interior.

Even before the destruction caused by the barbarian invasions in the 5th century A.D. (and even more so in the late Middle Ages when the region was the victim of raids by Arab pirates), coastal Etruria was already described as a desolate, inhospitable and unhealthy wasteland. Natural phenomena, such as the silting up of the river mouths which caused the plains to turn into swamps, favoured the spread of malaria. Pisa was the only Roman town, thanks to its favourable position at the mouth of the most important Tuscan valley and its natural harbour, that remained an urban settlement of any importance during the late Middle Ages. Several new towns grew up along the major communication route of the time, the Via *Francigena* or *Romea*, which connected central and western Europe to the capital of Christianity through the Cisa pass, Pontremoli, Lucca, Altopascio, Fucecchio, San Gimignano (later Poggibonsi), Siena, Radicofani and Acquapendente.

The importance of this road definitively moved the economic, cultural and demographic centre of Etruria towards the interior: a process which culminated in the 13th and 14th centuries when Florence asserted her supremacy by gaining control over the routes leading to the Appennine passes in the Mugello towards Bologna.

11. Map of settlements in Etruria in classical times.

12. Shard with a graffito (from Vado all'Arancio, Upper Paleolithic). Florence, Florentine Prehistorical Museum.

13. Funerary objects (from Vecchiano, Aeneolithic). Pisa, Institute of Anthropology.

THE PREHISTORICAL AGE

by Renata Grifoni Cremonesi

12

13

The earliest evidence of man in the region which is today Tuscany and Latium is given by some shards found near Bibbona and in the area around Livorno. Later, about 300,000 years ago, *Homo Erectus* lived in open-air settlements and used bifacial implements. During the Middle Palaeolithic period, we have evidence of large settlements of Neanderthal Man, who lived in Europe between 80,000 and 35,000 years ago and used chipped stone implements (Mousterian culture). The Upper Palaeolithic period, during which man acquired his modern physical appearance, is very well documented. In Tuscany there is evidence of all the different phases: from the Ulutian culture to the Aurignacian, from the Gravettian to the Epigravettian. At the end of the Würmian ice age, about 9,000 years ago, in a hot and dry climate, microlithic cultures began to spread. Evidence of these is found even at quite high altitudes on the Tuscan-Emilian Appennines and it is attributed to that era called the Mesolithic, which witnessed radical transformations of the habitat.

The transition to the Neolithic period is characterized primarily by the development of a productive economy, with the introduction of agriculture and animal husbandry, as well as by the spread of new technologies, such as pottery-making and the polishing of stone implements. The oldest Neolithic Italian culture, dating from about 7,500 years ago, is documented only by a few fragments of unbaked impressed pottery found at Pisa, on the island of Pianosa and at Pienza. Incised line pottery appears to have been more widely spread, and shards have been found over a wide area between the Po valley and Tuscany and Latium, in a timespan that goes from 6,200 to 5,400 years ago. Our evidence comes mostly from caves used as burial and worship sites; we have little documentation about the settlements. The Lagozza culture, dating from 4,700 years ago, spread primarily over the western Po valley; finds of polished black pottery in caves around Pisa and Siena attest its presence in Tuscany. This culture is evidence of the gradual transition to the metal ages, until the affirmation of the Aeneolithic cultures, derived probably from contact with Eastern Mediterranean peoples. The Aeneolithic period (2400-1800 B.C.) is well documented by a large number of tombs containing copper weapons, stone axes and hammers, and arrowheads, evidence of new ideologies and customs. While northern Latium and southern Tuscany are dominated by the Rinaldone culture with its typical tomb shaped like an artificial small grotto, the area around Siena and the Colline Metallifere (between Siena and the coast) use ditch graves and in northern Tuscany burial sites are in natural grottoes, more related to the Po valley and the Ligurian and Provençal cultures than to those of central and southern Tuscany.

During the Bronze Age (1600-1000 B.C.) the Appennine and sub-Appennine cultures flourish in southern Tuscany, Umbria and Latium: their economy is agricultural and pastoral. Also at this time, we have the appearance of the proto-Villanovan culture, which marks the end of this era.

The earliest stages of the Bronze Age are very scarcely documented. The Appennine culture, characterized by pottery decorated with spiral patterns, and the sub-Appennine culture, with pottery without decoration but with elaborate handles, are present in southern Tuscany and Latium.

Many important fortified centres spring up during the period of the proto-Villanovan culture; they bear witness to an increase in trade and the development of Bronze Age cultures towards early forms of urban communities.

THE ETRUSCAN PERIOD

by Marisa Bonamici

One can begin to speak of an Etruscan people with the advent of the so-called Villanovan culture (9th-8th centuries B.C.). During this period, the population lived in reed or wood huts; the tombs consisted of little wells dug in the ground containing biconical ossuaries and, in the later period (8th century), of inhumation of the deceased with personal objects.

Towards the middle of the 8th century B.C. an event that was to have an extraordinary effect on the Italian peninsula took place: the first Greek colonizers, coming from Chalcis and Eretria, set up trade bases in Campania. In their search for metals, they soon came into contact with Etruria, attracted by the mineral wealth of Elba and the area around Campiglia, the Colline Metallifere and the Tolfa Mountains. This was the beginning of a period of remarkable development for the Etruscans and, thanks to the metal trade, also of social differentiation. It is at this stage that the Etruscans acquire not only those luxury items that constitute the most remarkable aspect of the "Oriental" style tombs of the 7th century, but also the essential technological innovations in the field of metalworking and pottery and, especially towards the beginning of the 7th century, writing. An aristocratic class, consisting of those who controlled trade, was created and their role was to be fundamental throughout Etruscan history. Also at this time the population began to increase and gradually cities were formed—towards the end of the century in the more developed areas of southern Etruria, later in the northern part of the region.

The later history of the Etruscans is only the logical development of these beginnings: Etruria is active in the world of maritime trade and establishes a continuous and profitable commercial and cultural exchange with Greek and Oriental traders. At the same time, the development of its craftsmanship, throughout the 7th and 6th centuries, gives rise to a democratically-minded middle class, particularly in southern Etruria (Caere, Veii, Volsinii). This middle class is also responsible for the move towards colonization (beginning of the 5th century), which led to the founding of Capua in Campania and of Marzabotto and Felsina (Bologna) north of the Appennines.

In 474 B.C. the Etruscans were defeated by the Cumans and the Syracusans: this marked the beginning of the decline of their trading activities and, consequently, of their contact with the Greek world. But the recession only really affected the coastal towns—except Populonia—while the inland cities continued to thrive on agriculture and the sale of their manufactured objects to the centres north of the Appennines.

By the 4th century, with the invasions of the Gauls in the north and of the Samnites in Campania, Etruria was reduced once again to its original territory, but this brought the region a renewed prosperity. The population returned to the countryside and the aristocracy conquered new powers, very soon creating a relationship of conflict with the lower classes. The history of Etruria is from this time onward merely the history of its relationship with the growing power of Rome, beginning with the traumatic fall of Veii (396 B.C.) and culminating, after various wars and truces, with the separate alliances (*foedera*) that the Etruscan cities were forced to sign in the first half of the 3rd century. The terms of these alliances must have been very harsh. Livy gives a list of the tributes that Rome demanded of the Etruscan cities in 205 B.C., just before Scipio's expedition to Africa: wood and agricultural produce from Caere, Tarquinia, Volterra, Perugia, Chiusi and Roselle; iron from Populonia; arms, metal implements and grain from Arezzo.

During the 2nd century southern Etruria experienced an economic decline, for it was abandoned by the aristocracy who had settled in Rome. Northern Etruria, on the other hand, which was not abandoned by the aristocracy, was on the communication routes from Rome to the north and enjoyed a period of great prosperity. In 90 B.C. the Etruscans were granted Roman citizenship; this put an end to their apparent autonomy and marked the beginning of a new historical period.

14

15

16

17

14. Orvieto, Crocifisso del Tufo necropolis (6th-5th century B.C.).

15. Cerveteri, Banditaccia necropolis, area of the "Nuovi Scavi" (7th-6th century B.C.). This group of tumulus tombs, each of which contains the burial place of several members of a family clan, shows clearly the existence of an aristocracy.

16. Hut-shaped urn in bronze lamina with relief decorations (from Vulci, around the mid-8th century B.C.). Rome, Villa Giulia. This cinerary urn takes its shape from the houses of the Villanovan period, with an oval ground-plan and wooden beams.

17. Bronze statue of the Orator (from Pila, near Perugia, late 2nd or early 1st century B.C.). Florence, Archaeological Museum. The statue was a votive offering, as the inscription says, to the god Tec Sans from Avle Meteli, a member of the aristocracy from the area around Perugia.

THE ROMAN PERIOD

by Andreina Ricci

The systematic conquest of Etruria, begun by Rome in the 4th century, suffered several setbacks. After the fall of Veii in 396 B.C., the towns of Sutri and Nepi were also conquered in 382 B.C. Livy considered these towns "the barriers and gateways of Etruria." The reaction to these defeats by the other Etruscan cities was different: some, like Caere, signed alliances with Rome (Caere was granted the position of *civitas sine suffragio*, equality with Rome but with no right to vote); others organized a strong opposition, like Tarquinia and Falerii, who took arms against Rome in 358 B.C. and succeeded in forcing Caere to abandon her pro-Roman position and join the league of Etruscan cities.

Towards the end of the century, Volsinii and Perugia lead a new opposition against Roman expansionism. But the defeat at Sentinum in 295 B.C. marks the beginning of a series of victorious Roman campaigns against Etruscan cities, followed by the confiscation of most of their land and a reorganization of the communication routes. On the new conquered territories the Romans founded Castrum Novum and Pyrgi in 364 B.C., and Alsium and Fregenae in 245, conceived as military outposts controlling the coast (these are the years of the first war with Carthage) and those portions of Etruscan territory not yet entirely under Roman domination. The continuing battles in southern Etruria led to the destruction of Falerii and Volsinii (later rebuilt on different sites); but some Etruscan cities of the interior remained neutral, like Statonia and Saturnia which were considered prefectures and connected to Rome by the Clodian Way built before 225 B.C.

In the Etruscan cities of the north, however, Rome signed alliances with the local ruling classes and the only military interventions are more like police actions, requested by the local aristocracy, such as, for example, Rome's intervention in Arezzo in 302 B.C. in order to quell a revolt of the serfs. By the end of the 3rd century northern Etruria is connected to Rome by the Cassian Way. The process of colonization continues throughout the 2nd century, but the aim is no longer strictly military—the Gauls had been defeated in 225 B.C. New towns are founded: Saturnia in 183 B.C., Gravisca in 181 B.C. and Heba sometime between

18. View of the coast near Pyrgi.

19. Falerii Novi, city gate dedicated to Jupiter (3rd century B.C.).

20. Sutri, Amphitheatre (1st century B.C.?).

21. Nunziatella (near Cosa), the walls surrounding Villa delle Colonne (1st century B.C.).

21

167 and 157 B.C. The Roman aristocracy begins to take over the *ager publicus*, public land, a process which will lead, in the following century, to the spread of villas in the countryside. In northern Etruria, and especially in the area around Volterra, there are still large landed estates based on slave labour, whereas around Chiusi and Perugia new settlements spring up, varying in size from single farms to fairly large towns. This has usually been attributed to the social integration of part of the slaves. The Aurelian Way is prolonged at the end of the century (*Via Aemilia Scauri*) because of revolts in Liguria.

In the early 1st century (89 B.C.) almost all the populations of Italy are granted Roman citizenship. The Etruscan cities which had sided with Marius during the civil war are punished by the victorious Sulla with massacres, confiscation of land and destruction. Sulla also gives 120,000 of his soldiers land near Fiesole, Arezzo, Volterra and Chiusi. The population and land distribution in the region is thus radically altered, even though a few large family estates manage to survive—the *Cilnii* in Arezzo and the *Cecinae* in Volterra. This kind of colonization, aiming at distributing land to the veterans, continues throughout the century.

Under Augustus the whole of Etruria became part of the 7th Region and a new form of colonization, aimed at stopping the decline of some cities, was begun. This was then continued by his direct successors. The policy of restoration included also the rediscovery of ancient Etruscan traditions and during this period the region became the centre of the most important industries based on slave labour. From the 2nd century A.D. onward, most of the cities began to decline and, in the countryside, most of the settlements were abandoned. Only a few large estates were left (maritime villas), mostly imperial property. A description of the coast, made at the beginning of the 5th century by Rutilius Namatianus, a few years after the invasion of the Goths, shows the survival of only a few scattered communities.

THE MIDDLE AGES

by Riccardo Francovich

Tuscany, or Tuscia, in the Middle Ages was not a homogenous territorial or administrative unit. It consisted of the territories of Lucca, Luni, Pisa, Volterra, Pistoia and Florence, in the north, and of those of Siena, Arezzo, Chiusi, Perugia, Orvieto, as well as the royal lands donated to the Pope by Charlemagne—Sovana, Roselle, Populonia, Toscanella and Castro—in the south. After the Gothic domination, the Longobards gave the region a certain amount of unity, beginning in 570, setting up the duchy of Lucca, which under the Franks became a county. The first Frankish count was Boniface (812-823), who had come to Italy with Charlemagne and founded the dynasty which was to rule over the region for a century and a half. During this period the ties with Corsica and Sardinia were strengthened. Adalberto I (845-898) was called marquis of Tuscany, but it was not until the second half of the 10th century that the region became a marquisate. It was this institutional organization that allowed the development of that kind of autonomy which forms the basis of feudal seignories. The organization of the large feudal properties was based on the *curtis*, which denoted both the type of rural domination and the actual buildings housing this power. The basic characteristic of this system was the division of the estate in two parts: the part belonging directly to the lord (*pars dominica*) and the rest of the land which was divided into small plots, usually comprising a house lived in by slaves or freed men.

In the early Middle Ages Tuscany was in great decline. The areas in the valley of the Arno were swampy until at least the 10th century and only the small parts above the water were cultivated (such as the plain around Lucca). The area of the Maremma around Siena was almost entirely uninhabited and Bishop Giovanni (end of the 9th century) described the churches in ruins and the whole of Tuscany as a disease-ridden region—rather like Rutilius Namatianus's description, or that of Sidonius Apollinaris in 467.

The plains were abandoned and the population moved back to the hills, where they pursued pastoral activities. Agriculture, by now only just self-sufficient, was based on wheat, wine and olive oil. A document from Lucca, dating from 764, illustrates the basic diet: a loaf of wheat bread, a quarter of an amphora of wine and the same quantity of a mixture of beans and millet flour, with an occasional addition of meat. The settlements were very poor: huts and houses made of mud seem to have been the norm, as recent archaeological studies have proved. Groups of dwellings carved out of the rock were common in southern Tuscany as well as in a few other areas, such as the sandstone hills around Siena. Settlements of this kind lasted for a long time, in some cases till modern times.

The system of consular roads, which had remained efficient until the rule of Theodoric, soon declined under the Longobard domination, serving only as means of local communication. It was only later, with pilgrims and merchants, that they resumed their original importance.

The Longobards found two routes leading to Rome: the Aurelia, along the coast, and the Cassia, which went through Pistoia, Florence, Chiusi and Bolsena. But the Aurelia, exposed to dangers coming from the sea, passed through a desolate and swampy countryside. The Cassia, on the other hand, was abandoned not so much because of the increasing marshland in the Chiana valley, but because it was so close to the boundary with the Exarchate. This reduced the importance of the Tuscan mountain passes towards east and the major communication route became the pass of the Cisa further north. This is one of the reasons why Florence lost her supremacy over Lucca, which had become the major centre along the new route, called Via Francigena. The Via Francigena led from Luni to Lucca through Camaiore, then it reached the river Elsa south of San Miniato via Fucecchio, continuing on to Poggibonsi and Siena; then it followed the valley of the Arbia to Buonconvento, San Quirico and Radicofani and finally, through the valley of the Paglia, it reached Bolsena, Montefiascone and Viterbo. A north to south route that was to last a long time.

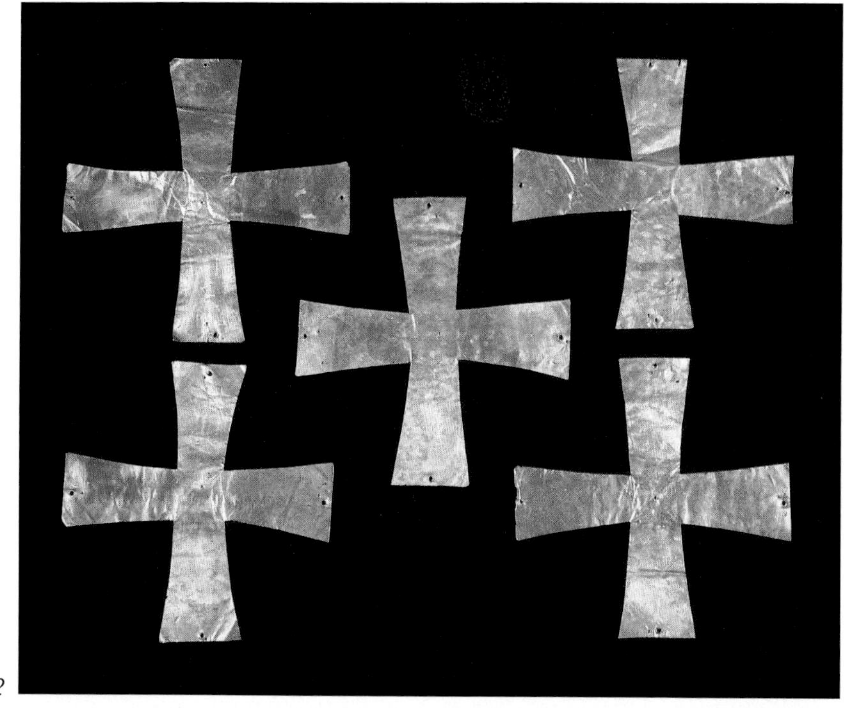

22

23

24

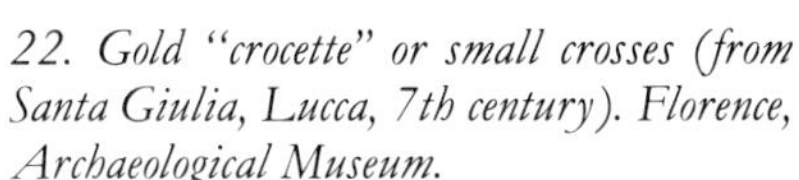

22. Gold "crocette" or small crosses (from Santa Giulia, Lucca, 7th century). Florence, Archaeological Museum.

23. Sovana, ciborium of the church of Santa Maria (8th-9th century).

24. "Byzantine" bronze belt buckles (from tomb 73 at Grangia, second half of the 7th century). Grosseto, Archaeological Museum.

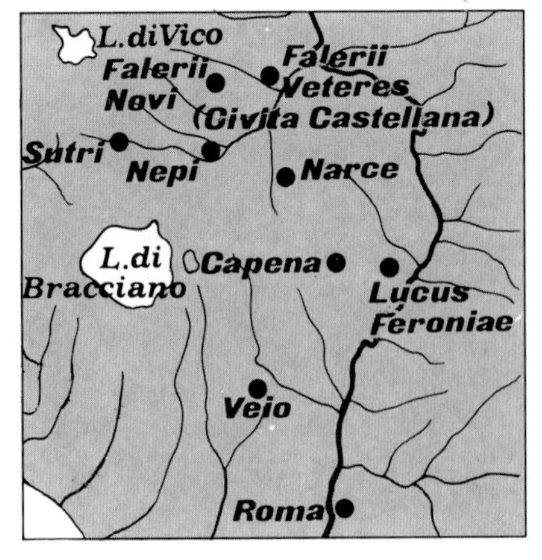

THE ARCHEOLOGICAL AREAS

VEII AND THE FALISCAN PLAIN

Finds from the upper Palaeolithic period come from the Cavernette Falische and from Vignanello (Pigorini and Villa Giulia Museums in Rome). The Neolithic is documented in the Grotto of Montevenere on the Lake of Vico—incised line pottery probably connected to worship practices—as well as in the Cavernette Falische and in the Vannaro Grotto at Corchiano (Villa Giulia). The Bronze Age is well represented by the village on the Appennines called Montevenere, by the bronze and iron objects found at Narce, by the proto-Villanovan settlements and tombs at Veii and by the pile-dwellings on Lake Bracciano (Villa Giulia).

The plateau of Comunità, the site first of villages and later of the city of VEII, and the necropolises on the surrounding hills and valleys have provided us with major finds of the Villanovan culture—thanks especially to the Anglo-Italian excavation of Quattro Fontanili. These finds have helped in the study of this culture in the rest of Etruria (objects at Villa Giulia and at the Museum of Civita Castellana). Also important is the 8th-century B.C. pottery from the Ciclades and Euboea (and the later imitations produced locally), which are the result of trade with the first Greek colonizers; Veii controlled the mouth of the Tiber and thus held a privileged position in dealings with the Greeks. This was in fact the primary reason of the conflict with Rome and Veii was the first victim of Rome's expansionist policy.

The first "Oriental" phase (first half of the 7th century) flourished here and the objects found in the tombs clearly show the influence of Caere and the Faliscan Plain (objects at the Archaeological Museum in Florence, at Villa Giulia and at the Pigorini Museum in Rome). There are very few finds of objects related to the aristocracy, among which a few burial sites and the recently discovered chamber tomb at Monte Oliviero, with an array of princely objects (at Villa Giulia), similar in composition to those found in the Regolini Galassi tomb in Caere. Also exceptional is the painted "Tomb of the Ducks" (second quarter of the 7th century), now open to the public at Riserva del Bagno: the frieze of little ducks is reminiscent of geometrical Etruscan ceramics showing Euboean influence. The "Chigi olpe" is also unique: it was produced and decorated on commission by Corinthian craftsmen around 650 B.C. (Villa Giulia). Among the more recent "Oriental" finds, only the Campana tomb at Monte Michele shows any autonomous artistic tradition. Its end wall is embellished by a painted decoration (animals on the lower level, and two knights accompanied by men on foot above) which shows a polychrome technique and a late "Oriental" style similar to the contemporary Etruscan-Corinthian ceramics.

The community of Veii became an urban settlement towards the beginning of the 6th century when a group of permanent constructions were built on the acropolis (Piazza d'Armi). At the centre stood a rectangular temple, which was abandoned at the end of the century when the sanctuary of Portonaccio, dedicated to *Menerva*

25. Clay statue of Apollo from the acroterion (from the sanctuary of Portonaccio at Veii, late 6th century B.C.). Rome, Villa Giulia.

25

26

27

26. Veii, Roman road.

27. Veii, excavations at the sanctuary of Portonaccio (late 6th century B.C.). In the foreground, the large water reservoir.

28. Veii, ruins of the Roman villa at Campetti. In the background, the water cistern.

29. The "Chigi olpe" produced by Corinthian craftsmen (from Veii, mid-7th century B.C.). Rome, Villa Giulia. On this side, starting at the top: battle scenes, procession of knights following a chariot, hunting scenes.

28

(Minerva), was built outside the city. At Portonaccio, just as at Campetti (see below), evidence of continuous religious practice until the the 1st century is provided by many ex-votos, some of which are of great interest, such as the one offered by the celebrated *Avile Vipiennas*, citizen of Vulci or the small statue depicting Aeneas carrying Anchises—an episode taken over by groups of Romans as a symbol of their move to the newly conquered city. The sanctuary, which is open to the public, consists of a central structure (probably a *cella* with *alae*) with, next to it, a large pond used in the religious ceremonies and filled by a network of little canals. In front there is a small building which contained an altar and the votive gifts. But the most interesting aspect of this monument are the large clay statues,

29

30

which originally stood on the peak of the roof, representing Apollo, Latona, Heracles and Hermes (Villa Giulia). They are the work of the sculptor from Veii, *Vulca*, famous in antiquity, who was also the author of the decoration of the temple of Jupiter on the Capitoline Hill in Rome.

The contemporary foundation, in the centre of the city, of the sanctuary of Campetti dedicated to the goddess *Vei* (who can be identified with the Roman Ceres), worshipped in Etruria and Rome by the lower classes, probably indicates a political supremacy of the plebeians. This perhaps explains why, although Latin sources refer to "kings" of Veii, the objects found in the 6th and 5th-century tombs are never very lavish. These "kings" were probably tyrannical figures and there may well have been laws banning excess luxury, based on Solon's legislation and inspired by equalitarian and anti-aristocratic sentiments. The city continued to prosper throughout the 5th century, thanks to its well-developed agriculture, as we can see by the surviving underground drainage conduits all over the countryside, among which the so-called Ponte Sodo (see p. 50), still visible today. It was in this period of prosperity that Veii was influenced by the classical Greek style, examples of which are the "Malavolta Head" and the statue of a young man, both in the manner of Polycleitus (from Portonaccio, now at Villa Giulia). According lo Livy, the city was conquered by the Romans in 396 B.C., after a ten-year siege. The Roman conquest was made easier by the fact that part of the league of Etruscan cities, ruled by an oligarchy, abandoned Veii because of its anomalous monarchy.

31

30. Fragment of a sculpted and painted head, probably Zeus (from Falerii 'Scasato', first half of the 4th century B.C.). Rome, Villa Giulia.

31. Impasto cup (from Narce, second half of the 7th century B.C.). Rome, Villa Giulia. Along the rims there are sculptural decorations: a man holding four horses and two horses' heads.

Prehistorical Implements

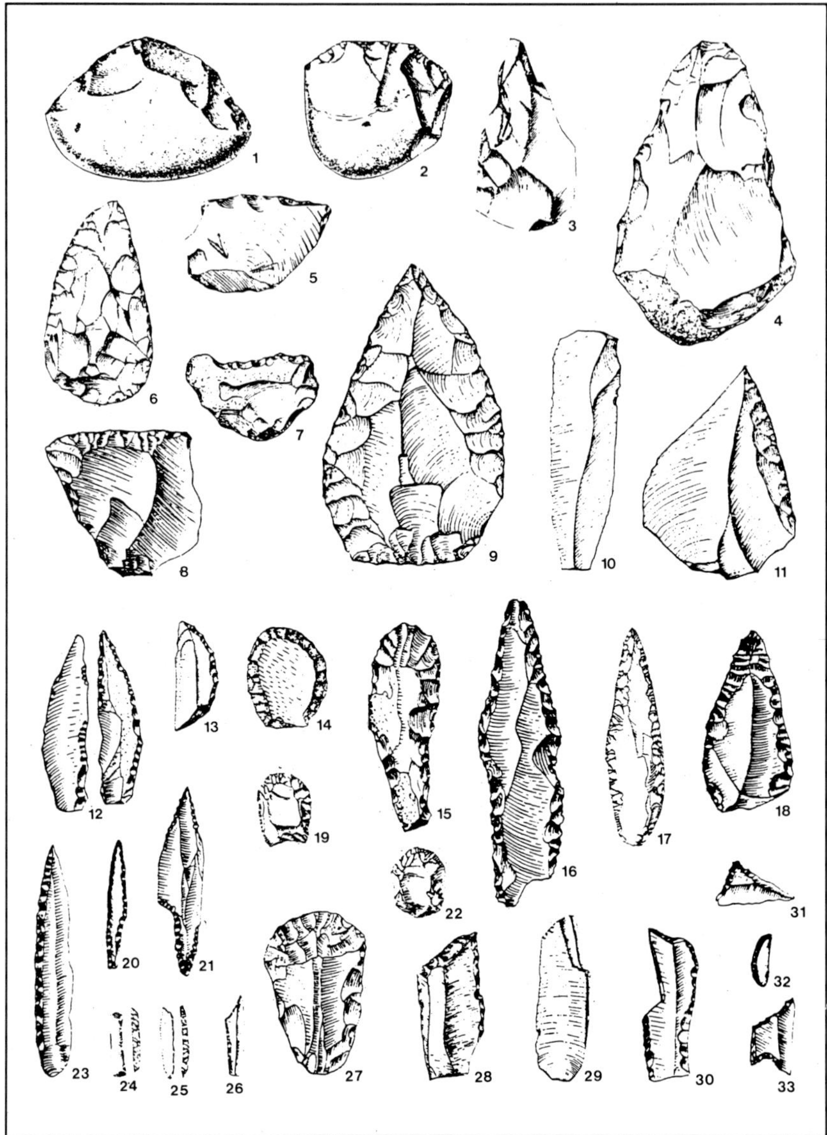

I

The first implements manufactured by man were simple shards, chipped at one end (choppers) found in Africa, and which date from two or two and a half million years ago; some have also been found in Europe. This elementary utensil gradually developed into the bifacial implement (*amigdala*), chipped probably with the aid of a stone hammer. The flakes were used as well, but gradually the chipping technique succeeded in producing flakes of a determinate shape; the earliest ones were wide and thick, the later ones, produced with a wood or bone billet, were thinner. During the Middle Palaeolithic more complicated procedures came to be used: a core of flint was roughly prepared and then regular shaped flakes were chipped off and retouched at the edges to be used as points and scrapers. In the Upper Palaeolithic, man refined these techniques even further; he managed to obtain long, thin blades providing a wide range of specialized tools, proving that the communities of hunters were involved in a variety of activities. Bone was also widely used during the Palaeolithic. The oldest tools that we know of are bifacials made of bone flakes found in Latium, but the use of this material was widespread in the Upper Palaeolithic: awls, gravers, points, harpoons, perforators, often decorated or sculpted. Unfortunately we have no evidence of objects produced in other materials (wood, leather, vegetable fibres, and so on) and we can only guess at the actual function of the stone tools. During the Mesolithic the predominant flint industry is that of pygmy flints or microliths in the shape of triangles, trapeziums and crescents, which were probably used as arrowheads. During the Neolithic, stone tools were made of obsidian (volcanic glass) as well as flint. Generally they were of regular shapes, frequently trapezoidal, and were often used as reaping-hooks; the first dressed stone bifacial arrowheads also appeared. A technological innovation were celts (ax or adz heads) edged by grinding and polishing. Bone continued to be used for points, needles, hooks and harpoons. Grindstones, used as early as the Upper Palaeolithic, became more widespread as agricultural activity developed: large pieces of sandstone or volcanic stone were used, with smaller ones as mullers. For weaving, Neolithic man used terracotta or stone spindles and loom weights; fragments of fabrics have been found in pile-dwellings. During the Aeneolithic we find stone arrowheads with tangs, retouched on both sides, with small nails to fix them to the handles, as well as flat axes and narrow points. During the Bronze Age, metal objects replaced stone ones almost entirely: we have found swords, daggers, points and also tools such as axes, sickles, saws and chisels. Bronze ornaments (brooches, necklaces and bracelets) and amber objects replace the previous shell, bone, stone or tooth ornaments. In the pile-dwellings of northern Italy a variety of wooden vases and other utensils have been found; these enable us to have a better picture of the complex agricultural and manufacturing activities of this period. The first examples of the wheel appeared at this time.

II

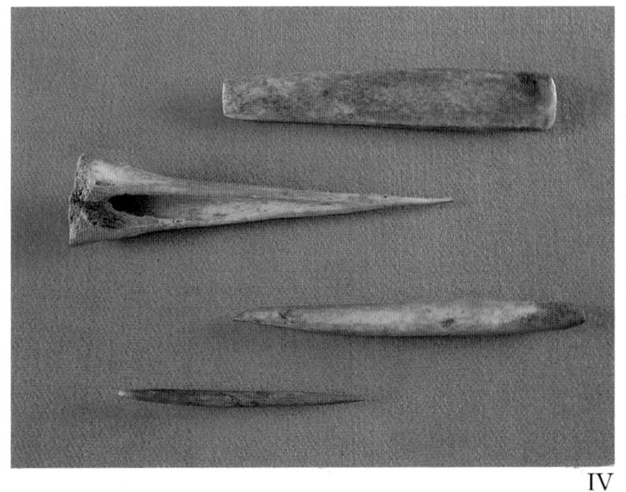

IV

V

III

VI

I. Reconstruction of prehistorical implements: shards from the Lower Palaeolithic (1-7), from the Middle Palaeolithic (8-11), from the Upper Palaeolithic (12-30), and from the Mesolithic (31-33).

II. Palaeolithic shard. Florence, Florentine Prehistorical Museum.

III. Two adzes in dressed stone (Neolithic). Pisa, Institute of Anthropology.

IV. Bone implements: spatula, point, spearhead (Neolithic). Pisa, Insitute of Anthropology.

V. Grindstone (Neolithic). Pisa, Institute of Anthropology.

VI. Copper adz (Aeneolithic). Pisa, Institute of Anthropology.

VII. Terracotta whorl for weaving (Neolithic). Pisa, Institute of Anthropology.

VII

32

34

33

32. Lucus Feroniae, the living quarters of the Volusii Villa (1st century B.C.).

33. Lucus Feroniae, mosaic floor of the peristyle of the Volusii Villa.

34. Lucus Feroniae, the basilica (1st century B.C.). In the foreground, the inlaid marble floor.

During its cultural development and later during the conflict with Rome, the only territory which remained allied to Veii was the Faliscan plain. This area, with the towns of FALERII, NARCE and CAPENA (in antiquity considered a colony of Veii), was inhabited by a non-Etruscan population who spoke an Italic language, Faliscan, similar to Latin. The finds in the tombs of this region from the 9th to the 6th century bear witness to a civilization very similar to contemporary Veii and southern Etruria, both in the form of the burial sites (cremation tombs in tufa stone containers, followed by shafts in tree-trunks and chamber tombs) and in the objects found in them (impasto, bronzes, bucchero, original Greek ceramics and imitations). An element, however, typical only of the Faliscan tradition is the influence derived from the Sabines and other inhabitants of Latium, visible in the impasto vases with animal figures and foliage, incised and incaved, dating from the 7th and 6th centuries (Villa Giulia).

The most remarkable period of development in this area took place in the 5th century, at a time when Falerii became a real urban settlement (and Narce was abandoned); the sanctuaries of Vignale and Scasato were built in the city, those of Sassi Caduti and Celle outside the walls. The latter was dedicated to Juno Curitis and the ruins of part of its structure have survived. Terracottas of great interest have been found on the sites of all these buildings (Villa Giulia). Just to mention a few: two fighting warriors, from Sassi Caduti (beginning of the 5th century); a bearded head in the style of Phidias's Zeus at Olympia; works influenced by the style of 4th-century Greek artists, like the statue of Apollo from Scasato, inspired by Lysippus's portrait of Alexander the Great, the two statues of a man and a woman inspired by Praxiteles, from Celle and Scasato, and the head of a man from Scasato in the manner of Skopas. In this artistic atmosphere, strongly influenced by Greece, towards the end of the 5th century a workshop producing red-figure ceramics was founded in Falerii. This workshop, probably set up by immigrant Attic artists, has left us such masterpieces as the krater of "the painter of Diespater" and that of "the painter of Aurora" (Villa Giulia).

In 394, after the defeats of both Veii and Capena, Falerii is forced to sign a truce with Rome which will lead, after various ups and

downs, to the rebellion of 241 ending with the complete destruction of the city.

After VEII was conquered by Furius Camillus in 396 B.C., the worship of Juno Regina was transferred to Rome and a large part of the conquered land was distributed to the Roman plebeians (an attempt at solving the conflict between patricians and plebeians). A class of small landowners was thus created and their presence is evident in the archaeological finds. The countryside appears to have been densely populated, while the cities were being progressively abandoned as early as the 2nd century. Later the villas, the centres of larger estates, replaced the smaller settlements established by the small-holders and farmers. The ruins of a grand late-republican villa are still visible near Anguillara. Some of the villas grew up within the cities themselves incorporating existing constructions. At the Campetti villa (1st century B.C.) a cistern and semi-circular nymphaeum are still visible. In front of the nymphaeum a black and white mosaic was found. The sanctuary of Portonaccio was used until the 1st century B.C. (as is shown by the votive offerings). Shortly after it was abandoned, a road was built across the site.

Augustus's project, followed also by his immediate successors, of reviving the declining city of Veii (and other centres of Etruria) led to the creation of the *Municipium Augustum Veiens*, which was embellished by several important buildings, such as the temples of Mars and of Victory, a public bath building (the ruins are known as the "Bagno della Regina") and a *porticus Augusta*, commissioned by Tiberius. Twelve Ionic columns of Carrara marble, discovered in 1912-17, are now visible in the atrium of Palazzo Wedekind in Rome (Piazza Colonna).

But, despite these attempts, the city progressively declined, while the surrounding countryside remained densely populated. The countryside here was in fact abandoned much later and much more slowly than elsewhere. The so-called "Muracci di Santo Stefano" (near Anguillara) are in fact the ruins of a 2nd-century A.D. villa, later converted into a place of Christian worship.

From the site of LUCUS FERONIAE (*Colonia Iulia Lucoferoniensis*), founded probably around the middle of the 1st century B.C., the

35. Lucus Feroniae, the amphitheatre (1st century B.C.).

36. Lucus Feroniae, the Aerarium (1st century B.C.).

37. Lucus Feroniae, warehouse counter with built-in dolium.

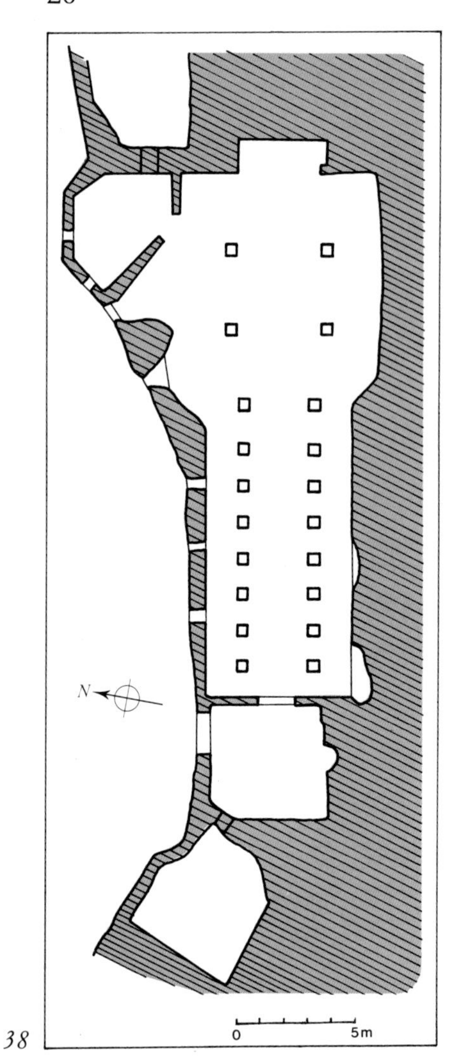

38. *Ground-plan of the mountain church of Santa Maria del Parto at Sutri.*

39. *Sutri, the mountain church of Santa Maria del Parto (6th century ?).*

whole valley of the Tiber is visible. The southern part of the plateau is taken up by the sacred wood of the goddess Feronia (of Sabine origin), protectress of animals. The worship of this deity is very ancient and the neighbouring populations (Latins, Sabines, Etruscans and Faliscans) gathered here. The settlement grew up at the edge of the sacred wood. The forum belongs to the earlier stage of the life of this city, before the arrival of the *Volusii Saturninii* family in Augustan times. Along the north-western side of the forum stood the basilica and the entrance to a small underground room where the colony's treasure (*aerarium*) was kept. At the foot of the basilica there are two small temples, and there were various shops along one of the long sides of the square. There are also the ruins of a bath building, probably built in the 1st century A.D., which continued to function until quite late, at least until the end of the 5th century. One can also see the remains of a house dating from the republican period and those of an amphitheatre which is very small and leads us to believe that the city was not densely populated. Near the amphitheatre the ruins of a public bath have been found. A visit to the *Volusii* villa, on the Autostrada del Sole, which has been largely preserved, is well worthwhile.

After the destruction of Falerii Veteres in 241 B.C., a certain amount of time elapsed before the new city, FALERII NOVI, was built in 220. The old city stood on the site of present-day Civita Castellana; the new one, a few miles away, on the site of today's Santa Maria di Falleri. It was rectangular in plan and sprang up around the Via Amerina which crosses it. The *insulae* are rectangular. The walls surrounding the town have watchtowers and gates. Inside, the ruins of a theatre have been found; outside the walls stand the remains of an amphitheatre, which was presumably built around the 1st century A.D. Many important engineering works took place in the course of the history of Falerii Novi, such as the bridge over the Amerina and the Fosso Tre Ponti acqueduct.

Unlike the majority of the cities of Etruria, this town was still thriving in the late-classical period.

The most well-known and widely spread types of rural settlements in Latium in the 8th and 9th centuries are the *domuscultae*, large landed estates administered by the Papacy and which had come into being thanks to bequests. Some of these have been studied both topographically and archaeologically: among them, Santa Rufina, not far from Rome, and Santa Cornelia, near Veii, where an early medieval church has come to light. It stands in the administrative centre of the estate, which was enlarged by Pope Hadrian I increasing the *fundus Capracorum*, donated in the 8th century to the deacon of Santa Maria in Cosmedin by *dux Eustachius*. We still know very little about the decline of these settlements in the plains, but their disappearance may be related to the dangers of the times (Moslem raids) and to the development during the 10th century of hilltop communities. These communities, a revival of pre-Roman customs, could not be reached by vehicles on wheels; they were naturally fortified and far removed from the major communication routes, in a region where the distances between the cities, such as Civita Castellana, Nepi and Sutri, were considerable.

Religious buildings dug out of the tufa stone are one of the more frequent characteristics of this phenomenon of hilltop communities, so common in northern Latium. The church of Santa Maria del Parto, west of the Cassian Way, near SUTRI, stands in an area where the Longobard occupation was shorter—Sutri was only conquered by Liutprand in 728—and its influence less radical, compared to the more central parts of their conquered territory. The church consists in a nave and two aisles separated by square pilasters and longitudinal arches. There is also a large flat-roofed presbytery with four pilasters. Inside, among very badly damaged frescoes dating from the 12th to 14th centuries, there are two figures in red (a dove with an olive branch and a fish) on the two pilasters near the presbytery, which can be dated to the 6th century thanks to their stylistic similarity with contemporary churches in southern Italy, in particular around Syracuse. The existence of rooms dug out of the rock nearby has suggested that there may have been catacombs on this site before the church, whereas it is almost certain that the pre-existing structures incorporated in the church were used as burial sites and as dwellings at the time of the Etruscans. The remains around the church were probably medieval houses.

VOLSINII

The Lower Palaeolithic is represented by shards found at Monte Peglia, the Middle by those found near Orvieto and the Upper by the Tane del Diavolo (Devil's Lairs) at Parrano (Archaeological Museum, Perugia). The Neolithic period is well represented both at the Grotta Bella of Montecastrilli and at the wells called Pozzi della Piana at Titignano, connected to the worship of water. The Aeneolithic has yielded finds at Terni Acciaierie (Pigorini Museum in Rome and Civic Museum in Terni), at the Rinaldone necropolis (Montefiascone) and in the tomb of Fosso Conicchio (Pigorini Museum). The Bronze Age is represented by Appennine and sub-Appennine materials found at the Tane del Diavolo, Grotta San Francesco at Titignano, Pozzi della Piana and Grotta Bella.

On the territory that by the end of the 6th century was under the direct rule of VOLSINII (the present Orvieto), in other words the area between the north and east shores of Lake Bolsena and the Tiber and the Paglia, there is evidence of the Villanovan culture both in the village of Gran Carro and in Volsinii itself. The village of Gran

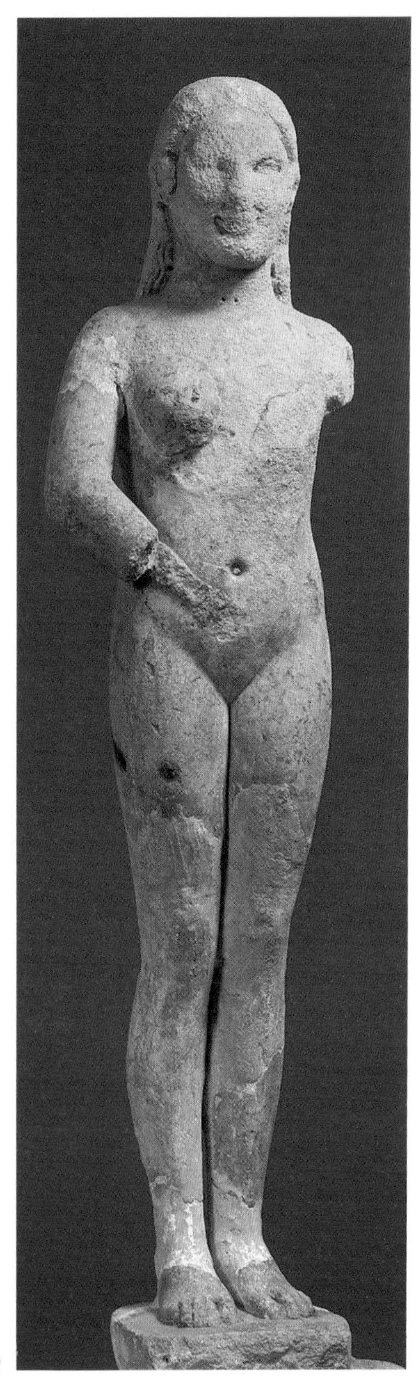

40

40. Oriental-Greek marble statue (around the end of the 6th century B.C.). Orvieto, Civic Museum. This statue of a naked goddess was the object of worship in the sanctuary of the Cannicella necropolis.

41. Bronze votive statue of a warrior offering a libation (from Todi, early 4th century B.C.). Vatican, Gregorian Etruscan Museum.

Carro is now under the water of the lake, near the east shore (the finds are in Bolsena and at Villa Giulia). The finds at Volsinii are in the Faina Museum; one can also visit the excavation of the 6th-5th century necropolises under the church of Sant'Andrea. During the period of the "Oriental" style, Volsinii was not one of the cities that imported precious objects and no artifacts indicating the existence of an aristocracy have come to light.

From the first half of the 6th century we find evidence in Volsinii of an organized urban community, but one which is particularly "democratic" in its set-up, a fact revealed primarily in the necropolis of Crocifisso del Tufo (open to the public). Here, the tombs are all similar in shape, size and quality of objects; they appear to have been laid out according to a strictly planned design and each one is identified by the name of the owner (objects in the Faina Museum and in the Palazzo dei Papi in Orvieto, together with an exhibition explaining the recent restorations). At this time the first craftsmen's workshops were set up and the products (impasto, bucchero, bronze vases) were sold to the neighbouring towns, Grotte Santo Stefano, Grotte di Castro, Civita del Fosso d'Arlena, Celleno, Bagnoregio, which nonetheless appear to have been economically independent.

By the second half of the century, Volsinii had become a prosperous city, thanks to its geographical position enabling it to control the Tiber and Chiana valleys, and thanks also to organized agriculture on the fertile plain. By this stage Orvieto was involved in the trade of Greek-Oriental artistic products, among which one must mention the famous "Venus" (Civic Museum, within the Faina Museum). It comes from the sanctuary at the centre of the Cannicella necropolis, which was dedicated to the goddess *Vei* here given the appearance of a funerary Aphrodite, a custom common in Greece. The production of bronze objects is also interesting: vases for common usage, objects of great artistic value in a Ionic style, such as foils for the decoration of carts (the so-called Ferroni foils from Todi, in the Archaeological Museum in Florence, and the bronzes from Castel San Mariano, partly now in the Archaeological Museum in Perugia) and small sculptures like the so-called Mars from Ravenna (in the Museum in Leyden). Objects of this kind were widely exported to Umbria, Romagna, Emilia and to Piceno. By this time Volsinii had won political supremacy over the area and this caused the decline and even abandon of some of the smaller settlements, such as the neighbouring citadel of Acquarossa ; border towns, on the other hand, were strengthened.

During the second half of the 5th century and the beginning of the 4th, the local workshops were influenced by the style of Phidias. Examples of this are the architectural terracottas of the temple of Belvedere (the excavation is open to the public), those found at the Cannicella necropolis and in Via San Leonardo (Faina Museum) and the bronze statue of Mars found in a sanctuary near Todi (now in the Gregorian Museum in the Vatican).

In the 4th century, some powerful land-owning families had underground tombs built for themselves outside the city. Among these, the Golini tombs at Settecamini and the Hescanas tomb at Porano, decorated with paintings praising the family and filled with

41

42

43

44

luxurious personal objects (now in the Palazzo dei Papi). This seems to indicate a prevalence of the countryside and of the aristocracy over the city, which must eventually have led to the civil strife mentioned in the sources. This paved the way for the Roman army's conquest of the city in 264 B.C. The inhabitants that survived were moved to a new city and the worship of Vertumnus, common to all Etruscans, was transferred to Rome. The conquering consul, M. Fulvius Flaccus, celebrated the event offering a group of bronze statues to the sanctuary of Sant'Omobono in Rome, as war booty. The tufa bases with the commemorative inscriptions have survived.

There is practically no mention of VOLSINII in our sources after the Roman conquest. The city only resumed a certain importance in the 6th century A.D. when it is mentioned in the writings of Paul the Deacon and Pope Gregory the Great. The only remains worthy of mention are the fragments of mosaics in the crypt of the church of Sant'Andrea.

VOLSINII NOVI, which replaced the old Volsinii (Orvieto) like Falerii Novi re-

42. Sarcophagus from Torre San Severo, from a tomb belonging to the agrarian aristocracy (around the mid-4th century B.C.). Orvieto, Civic Museum. On the long side, Achilles sacrifices the Trojan prisoners to the Manes of Patroclos; on the short side, Ulysses sacrifices a ram before the entrance to Hades.

43. Two ceramic amphoras, with relief decorations showing a battle of the Amazons (early 3rd century B.C.). Orvieto, Civic Museum. This type of vase, produced first at Volsinii and later at Volsinii Novi, is evidence of the continuity between the two towns.

44. Architectural terracotta from the aristocratic residence at Acquarossa, with a banquet scene (around the mid-6th century B.C.). Viterbo, Civic Museum.

The Language and Origins of the Etruscans

The Etruscan language, often mistakenly considered the most mysterious aspect of the so-called "Etruscan mystery," is in fact only partially understood. This does not mean that Etruscan inscriptions are not legible and, in the vast majority of cases, perfectly understandable. It means that it is a language which has not come down to us through a manuscript tradition, and is therefore known almost exclusively from epigraphs, most of which are funerary inscriptions offering only a restricted and repetitive range of information.

So far as we know, Etruscan is not an Indo-European language; it has phonetic and morphological connections with the language documented at Lemnos by an inscription dating from the late 6th century B.C. It would seem likely that Etruscan and Lemnian are the last relics of an ancient language common to the whole Mediterranean region.

Modern research makes no use of etymological methods, based on the comparison of Etruscan with other known languages. It studies the language on the basis of internal evidence provided by the texts themselves, and has obtained remarkable results in the understanding of the onomatological formulas, now perfectly clear, of many grammatical structures and of some syntactical constructions.

What we have said so far implies a clear distinction between the concept of language and the concept of alphabet, which consists only in a system of signs expressing the language itself. The Etruscan alphabet presents no problem; it is perfectly readable, for it is basically simply the Greek alphabet brought over by the Euboean colonizers, with a few adjustments. It began to be used in the early 7th century and, since it was an instrument of trade, at first it was used only by the aristocracy. Later, with the birth of urban communities, writing was taught in the temples, such as the Portonaccio temple at Veii, and began to be used to record public events (see the *lamina* of Pyrgi), lists of magistrates, and so on. At the same time, the practice of writing spread, until in the 2nd century in the territory of Chiusi and Perugia even the cinerary urns of slaves and freed men were normally inscribed with the names of the deceased.

I

II

III

IV

The "problem" of the origins of the Etruscans is in fact a false problem, invented by 19th-century historians inspired by the myth of nationalism. Ancient historians had already pointed to the origins of the Etruscans. According to Herodotus, the Greek 5th-century B.C. historian, they came from Lydia before the Trojan war (13th century B.C.); according to Dionysius of Halicarnassus, who lived at the time of Augustus, the Etruscans had always been in Etruria. These two theories have given rise to two different schools of thought: on the one hand there are those who see the Etruscan "Oriental" style as evidence of their Oriental origin, on the other those who consider the isolation of the Etruscan language proof of the existence of this people in the region before the migration of all other populations. Another trend of modern scholarship has advanced the theory that the Etruscans came from the north, producing as evidence the similarity of the Villanovan culture to that of the northern "urn fields." Faced with these three different hypotheses, none of them without contradictions, in 1947 Massimo Pallottino presented the problem in a new light. Pallottino claimed that it was wrong to approach the problem of the birth of a population from the point of view of "place of origin," as the ancients did. On the contrary, we must study civilizations in terms of "formation" and look to the historical development of the Etruscans.

V

VI

I. Ivory tablet showing the Greek alphabet, from right to left (from the Circolo degli Avori at Marsiliana d'Albegna, 650-625 B.C.). The tablet was part of the collection of personal objects found in a tomb; it indicates that writing in this period was the prerogative of the aristocracy.

II-IV. Gold laminas from the sanctuary at Pyrgi; the first to the left has a Phoenician inscription, the other two are in Etruscan (late 6th century B.C.). Rome, Villa Giulia. The inscriptions record that the king of Caere, Thefarie Velianas, dedicated Temple B to the goddess Uni.

V. Inscribed boundary stone, recording the agreement between the Velthina and Afuna families reached after a territorial dispute (from the area around Perugia, early 2nd century B.C.). Perugia, Archaeological Museum.

VI. Lead lamina from Magliano (5th-6th century B.C.). Florence, Archaeological Museum. The inscription is spiral-shaped and covers both sides; the content is rather obscure, but since it records the names of deities it may have been a devotional object.

placed Falerii (Civita Castellana), was founded on the shores of Lake Bolsena in 264 B.C. The new colony had control over such important communication routes as the Via Cassia and the new Via Traiana and this accounts for its status. Some families, originally from Volsinii Novi, became very important in Rome. There are only a few ruins of buildings of the republican period, in particular the forum and the theatre (the latter was discovered only thanks to aerial photographs). Among the constructions dating from the Flavian period we must mention the amphitheatre and a new forum (paved with marble slabs), and the basilica that opened onto it. This basilica was transformed into a Christian church in the 4th century A.D. and remains of catacombs (4th-5th centuries) have also been found. This indicates that, unlike other towns of Etruria, Volsinii Novi did not undergo a process of depopulation during the early and middle imperial age. The remains of two private houses, dating from the republican period (2nd century B.C.), are most interesting: each one has its own small sanctuary dedicated to Dionysus, which shows how widely spread the cult of the mysteries and their rites was even in private homes. These small places of worship were destroyed around the second half of the 2nd century A.D., after the Roman senate had banned the celebration of Bacchanalia in 186 B.C.

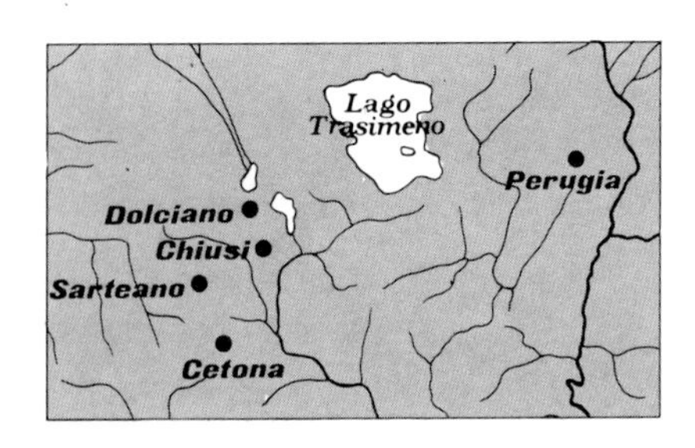

CHIUSI AND PERUGIA

The Lower Palaeolithic is represented in the region of CHIUSI only by a bifacial implement at Montepulciano; the Middle Palaeolithic, by finds in the Grotta di Gosto and in the Grotta Lattaia and Grotta San Francesco on Mount Cetona (Archaeological Museum, Perugia). The Neolithic period is well represented in all its stages: the village of Pienza with pottery with impressed patterns, the Grotta dell'Orso at Sarteano with incised line pottery (Archaeological Museum, Florence), the Grotta Lattaia with pottery of various traditions (Archaeological Museum, Perugia). Evidence of the Aeneolithic period is found in all the above-mentioned grottoes and in the Buca del Rospo at Cetona (Antiquarium, Cetona) and at Spedaletto near Pienza (Archaeological Museum, Florence). The finds from the Bronze Age are very abundant, especially in the Grotta dell'Orso at Sarteano and in the grottoes of Belverde at Cetona, where there are remains of tombs, fireplaces, wheat storage, belonging to all the different stages of the Bronze Age (Archaeological Museum, Perugia). On top of Mount Cetona and at Casa Carletti there are two fortified proto-Villanovan settlements.

The Lower and Middle Palaeolithic are represented in the territory of PERUGIA by bifacial implements and Mousterian shards found around Perugia, Lake Trasimeno and Norcia; the Upper Palaeolithic by shards found near Perugia and by the small stone statue known as the "Trasimeno Venus."

The Neolithic period is represented only by the Norcia hut (Archaeological Museum, Perugia). For the Aeneolithic, we have the ditch tomb from Marsciano (Civic Museum, Bologna). Bronze Age remains are more abundant, including the proto-Villanovan necropolises of Monteleone di Spoleto (Archaeological Museum, Florence) and Panicarola, and the objects in gold and bronze from Gualdo Tadino (Archaeological Museum, Perugia).

In the territory of CHIUSI, broadly speaking between Lake Trasimeno and Mount Amiata, from the Villanovan period through to the 7th century the population was scattered and did not tend to form urban-type communities (Chiusi, Chianciano, Sarteano, Cetona, Castelluccio di Pienza, Castiglione del Lago, Dolciano). The burials were individual, in shafts and in biconical ossuaries, and later (7th

century) in anthropomorphic jars and ossuaries (canopic urns); the rituals did not change and there is no sign of inhumation or aristocratic differentiation (objects in the museums of Chiusi, Siena and Florence). All this indicates an economy and a social organization based entirely on agricultural activity—considerably backward compared to the developments of southern Etruria.

It is only at the end of the 7th century that we find the first chamber tombs with multiple graves; they are placed around the future centre and are thus evidence of a rising aristocracy moving towards urban organization. The personal objects found in them are frequently lavish: bronze ossuaries placed on thrones (see the example from Dolciano in the Museum at Chiusi, with the head of the canopic urn, which may not be related to it), Etruscan-Corinthian ceramics and luxury items imported from southern Etruria (see, for example, the ivory pyx from the Pania, now in Florence). From the first half of the 6th century onwards, the local artistic market is more and more dominated by importations, such as the famous François krater, commissioned from the Attic painter Kleitias and painted around 550 B.C. (Archaeological Museum, Florence), and by the advent of craftsmen from southern Etruria, such as the ones from Vulci who manufactured stone funerary statues (sphinxes, lions, female figures, in the museums of Chiusi and Florence). By the second half of the century, Chiusi experienced all the typical phenomena that accompany the growth of a city, from the development of craftsmanship to the military control of the countryside, and the abandoning of the scattered small communities (such as Dolciano, Sarteano, Cetona). The first to be abandoned was the aristocratic citadel of MURLO, in the upper valley of the Ombrone, on the border between Chiusi's territory and that of Rusellae. Here, the recent American excavation has brought to light a square-plan building with an inner courtyard, decorated with splendid architectural terracottas (Palazzo Pubblico, Siena). The building had been intentionally abandoned in 525, at the same time as the birth of the city and the rise to power of King Porsenna, who first began Chiusi's expansionist policy. Chiusi also must have taken part in the foundation of Marzabotto, since some distinctive graphic symbols are used only in these two towns. By the sec-

45. Stone cinerary urn, with a relief decoration showing a banquet scene (from Chiusi, 520-500 B.C.). Florence, Archaeological Museum.

46. Incised line ceramics (from Grotta dell'Orso at Sarteano, Neolithic). Florence, Archaeological Museum.

47. Appennine culture ceramics (from Grotta dell'Orso at Sarteano, Bronze Age). Florence, Archaeological Museum.

48. Bowls (from Antro della Noce, Cetona, Bronze Age). Florence, Archaeological Museum.

49

50

51

49. Murlo, excavations of the aristocratic villa (around 580 B.C.).

50. Canopic urn from the Mieli Servadio collection (from Castelluccio di Pienza). Chiusi, National Museum. As often happened in Chiusi in the 19th century, this urn was put together using objects that bear no relationship to each other: a bronze ossuary (end of the 7th century), a terracotta head (end of the 6th century) and a terracotta throne.

ond half of the 6th and the beginning of the 5th centuries the local artistic production appears to be well-organized in workshops and, except for the painted tombs done by craftsmen from Tarquinia (the Tomb of the Monkey is open to the public), consists in canopic urns, heavy bucchero and above all local stone funerary monuments (inscribed stones, sarcophagi, urns) decorated with banquet scenes, dances and ceremonies related to the funeral ritual.

After the end of the 6th century the tradition of the canopic urns was replaced by local stone sculpted ash urns, influenced by Greek art in its various stages: from the Ionic to the classical (see the famous "Mater Matuta" and the two sarcophagus lids with a couple at a banquet in the Archaeological Museum in Florence).

The prosperity of the city, which derived both from the control over the Chiana valley and from agricultural activities (see, for example, the legend of Arruns who went to sell wine, oil and figs to the Gauls) continued in the 4th century, in the Hellenistic period and through the whole of the 2nd century—and was accompanied by a remarkable artistic production. In the first half of the 4th century a tradition of red-figure ceramic was set up; from the end of the century onwards, specialized craftsmen began to create sarcophagi and urns with relief decorations in pure Hellenistic style (museums of Florence, Chiusi and Siena). An interesting example of this style is the tomb of Pellegrina (open to the public), which also offers an insight into the organization of the aristocracy.

In the 2nd century, probably as a result of the revolts of 196 B.C., large numbers of slaves were set free and were granted small plots of land. New family names began to appear and, in the territory around Chiusi, the small countryside underground tombs were filled with little terracotta urns, made from moulds and decorated with scenes related to peasant beliefs.

The territory of PERUGIA, broadly speaking between the eastern shore of Lake Trasimeno and the Tiber, developed more or less along the same lines as that of Chiusi. We know very little of the

52

53

54

51. Sculpted stone group, with the deceased shown reclining at a banquet next to a female demon (Lasa) unrolling the scroll of his destiny (end of the 5th century B.C.). Florence, Archaeological Museum. The sculpture shows how closely the workshops in Chiusi were in contact with classical Greek styles.

52. Perugia, Palazzone necropolis, Tomb of the Volumni, central chamber with the urns of the members of the family. At the centre, the urn of the founder Arnth Velimna (second half of the 3rd century B.C.); to the far left the urn of P. Volumnius (Augustan period), showing that the tomb was re-used by a distant descendant of the original family.

53-54. Perugia, the city gates dedicated to Augustus and Mars (3rd-2nd century B.C.). Both these gates were originally built by the Etruscans and later modified by the Romans.

Villanovan period and of the 7th century. By the second half of the 6th century we have evidence of powerful aristocratic strongholds in the countryside, documented by the finds at San Valentino (now in Munich) and Castel San Mariano (partly in Munich, partly in Perugia). These aristocrats commissioned the bronze decorations for their carts and other prestige items from the workshops of Chiusi and Orvieto, as well as from southern Etruria. The chamber tombs, dating from about 500 B.C., of the Palazzone necropolis (an Antiquarium there is open to the public) and the use of writing indicate the birth of an urban organization, which reveals its cultural debt to Chiusi through the imported bucchero vases and the sarcophagus of Sperandio (Archaeological Museum, Perugia).

Although we have little documentation for the 4th century, the importation from Chiusi of the bronze sarcophagus, in the manner of Phidias, now in Leningrad, indicates a growing prosperity. In the 3rd and 2nd centuries an even greater degree of prosperity is shown by the construction of the city walls (Porta Marzia and Porta di Augusto) and by the growth of the necropolises. The tombs are mainly formed by several chambers, each containing many little urns, pro-

The Banquet in Etruria

In Etruscan artistic production the theme of the banquet reappears constantly: what is its meaning, what is the ideology behind these representations, in all their different contexts? The earliest representation of a banquet in Etruscan art is the one on the cinerary urn from Montescudaio, where the deceased, waited on by a maidservant, sits on a throne before a table prepared for a feast, according to the customs of the time (around the middle of the 7th century) in Greece and the Orient. The scene is clearly a reference to the age-old custom of the funeral banquet, held by the relatives and at which the deceased was believed to be present. Towards the middle of the 6th century, it became the custom in Greece to take part in banquets lying on beds, surrounded by music and dance; this practice, common only to the élite, was considered a sign of prestige. The scenes on the architectural reliefs found at Murlo and Acquarossa are of this kind, and the banquet takes on the function of self-portrayal of the exclusive aristocratic caste.

The representations of banquets on the 6th and 5th-century funeral monuments, such as the painted tombs at Tarquinia or the reliefs at Chiusi, obviously had the same function: to record the moment in which the representatives of the aristocracy were united around the deceased in the cerimonial feast, thus stressing their solidity and power.

From the late 5th century onwards, this kind of banquet is sometimes replaced by a banquet taking place in the Elysian fields, as is the case in some late painted tombs (Orco, Scudi and Golini). Here we have a blend of the two meanings of the scene—the aristocratic and the eschatological. The latter meaning is particularly obvious in the figures of the deceased, especially in the cinerary urns and on the lids of urns and sarcophagi found at Chiusi (4th-3rd century). They are portrayed with crowned heads and bare chests, attributes normally associated with heroes, far removed from the world of the living.

I

I. Cinerary urn from Montescudaio, detail of the lid (650-625 B.C.). Florence, Archaeological Museum. The deceased is portrayed seated on a throne at a banquet, attended to by a maidservant.

II. Fresco showing a banquet scene, from the Tomb of the Leopards at Tarquinia (first half of the 5th century B.C.).

III. Reconstruction of a banquet. The drawing shows various elements taken from Etruscan portrayals of banquets. In a lavish and splendid room, the participants lie (in the case of the men) or sit (in the case of the women) on couches, while a musician plays the flute.

II

III

55

56

57

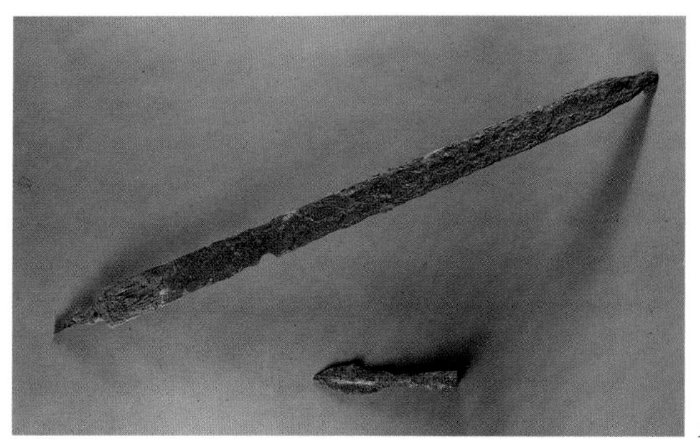
58

duced locally in Hellenistic style (many examples in the museum). Exceptional in this sphere are the tomb of the Volumni (*Velimna*, in Etruscan), in which six splendid 3rd-century urns and one from the Augustan period have been preserved (on view in the Palazzone necropolis), and the recently discovered tomb of the *Cae Cutu*, with the sarcophagus of the founder (second half of 3rd century) and the urns of the other members of the family down to the 1st century B.C.

By this time the countryside was characterized by numerous settlements, indicating intensive cultivation of the land. An inscribed stone from the 2nd century, found at Pian Castagneto (now in the Archaeological Museum, Perugia), records the agreement between the *Velthina* family and the *Afuna* family regarding a border controversy. Also from the countryside—from the valley of Sanguineto near Lake Trasimeno or from Pila, southwest of Perugia—is the famous bronze statue known as The Orator (Archaeological Museum, Florence, see p. 13). The inscription tells us that this is a donation to a sanctuary by *Avle Meteli* (Aulus Metellus), dating from around the end of the 2nd century, just before the Etruscans, like the rest of the Italic peoples, were granted Roman citizenship.

After the last great battle between Romans and Etruscans at Sentinum in 295 B.C., CHIUSI fell under Roman domination. In the 2nd century the city witnessed a revolt of the serfs (which involved Arezzo as well). It appears that during the 1st century Sulla granted his civil war veterans land around the city. From then on, the inhabitants were divided between *Clusini veteres* (old inhabitants) and *Clusini novi* (the new colonizers). We know very little of the life of the city during the imperial period. Some buildings dating from the Roman

59

55. Jugs from tombs around Chiusi (first half of the 7th century). Chiusi, Archaeological Museum.

56-59. Early medieval objects from the Arcisa necropolis. Chiusi, Archaeological Museum. Gold "crocette" or small crosses (56); shield studs (57); sword and spearhead (58); silver fibula in the second style (59).

period have been found under the cathedral (a large cistern with several aisles still exists under the bell tower); some inscriptions and sculptures are preserved in the local museum. The presence of the Christian catacombs at San Mustiola and Santa Caterina, on the outskirts of the city, would seem to indicate that the city was fairly important in the 4th and 5th centuries A.D.

As early as the 2nd century B.C., in the territory of Chiusi and that of Perugia the number of country settlements had increased probably because the slaves had been freed. Unlike southern Etruria, where the countryside was divided into large landed estates based on slave labour, here the serfs had been granted freedom and land after the great revolts they had led.

Since PERUGIA had sided with Antony in the civil war, in 40 B.C. it was conquered and sacked by the victorious Octavian (*bellum Perusinum*). Augustus granted the city privileges and promoted her reconstruction: the Porta di Augusto dates from this time although the inscriptions were added later. One of these inscriptions recalls that the city was granted *ius coloniae* (colonial rights) under Trebenianus Gallus (mid 3rd century A.D.), a privilege that at the time was only nominal and probably due to the fact that it was the emperor's birthplace.

CHIUSI lay on the old Cassian Way and was the seat of a diocese as early as the 4th century. It became Longobard later than the cities further north, since it was fairly close to the boundary with the Byzantines, who had occupied Perugia and the islands on Lake Trasimeno. We still know very little about the town in the early Middle Ages, or about the countryside where the traces of the occupation are visible primarily in the lavish tombs, among which the one that was excavated between 1913 and 1914 at Arcisa. In 1933 other tombs came to light near the barracks of the Carabinieri and, more recently, others still in the centre of the town and under the cathedral (founded around the 6th century). Among the objects found at Arcisa, and now visible in the museum, we must mention: jewellery decorations for belts (8th century), gold crosses, *spathae* (swords) and shields, a splendid fibula with a decoration consisting of a human head surrounded by animal heads. Some of the tombs also contained pottery: late classical red impasto jugs, confirming the absence of purely Longobard artistic productions.

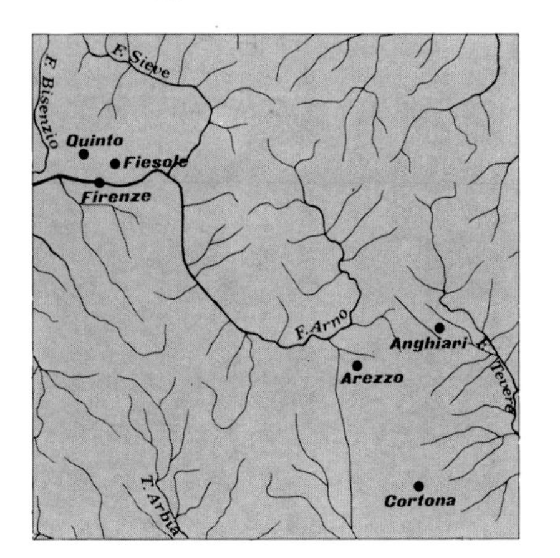

AREZZO, FIESOLE AND FLORENCE

The Lower Palaeolithic is represented by bifacial implements found in the valley of the Arno; the Middle and Upper Palaeolithic are documented by various remains of communities; worthy of note is the skull found at Olmo ("Cranio dell'Olmo") last century, casts of which are now to be seen in the Archaeological Museum of Arezzo, the Prehistorical Museum of Florence and the Archaeological Museum of Perugia. The Neolithic period is documented only by axes and adzes in dressed stone found on the surface; the Aeneolithic, by tombs of the Rinaldone culture at Marciano della Chiana and at Battifolle (Archaeological Museum, Arezzo). The finds documenting the Bronze Age are very few, among them the two swords from Frassineto and Terontola (Archaeological Museum, Arezzo).

Bifacial implements have been found at Montelupo and in the Pesa valley; Mousterian objects come from the Mugello. Shards documenting the Middle and Upper Palaeolithic have been found at Fucecchio, Prato, Troghi and in the Pesa valley. Finds from the Neolithic period are very few; the Aeneolithic is re-

60

62

60. The terracotta frame of the pediment of a temple (from Arezzo, piazza San Jacopo, around 480 B.C.). Arezzo, Archaeological Museum. The relief decoration shows battle scenes.

61. Fiesole, Etruscan temple. In the foreground, the stairs leading to the entrance. Originally built in the 3rd century B.C. and rebuilt, on the same ground-plan, in the 1st century B.C.

62. Quinto Fiorentino, Mula tholos tomb, the interior looking towards the entrance (630-600 B.C.). The false vault is created by rows of progressively projecting stone slabs.

61

presented by a tomb at Montespertoli and by remains found on the surface. Finds from the Appennine culture come from Dicomano; the sub-Appennine culture is represented by the finds at Fiesole and the three huts of Stabbia (Archaeological Museum and Prehistorical Museum, Florence).

The towns of northern inland Etruria, between Cortona and Fiesole, along the Arno and Chiana valleys, all experienced a similar development at the time of the Etruscans. They were all on the major route leading north, beyond the Appennines, and, except for Arezzo, developed into proper urban communities relatively late. The archaic period is represented in the territories of Arezzo and Cortona by lavish tombs, such as the two "melons" at Sodo and at Camucia containing remarkable "Oriental" style objects. These tombs were used between the end of the 7th and the 4th centuries and indicate the presence of aristocracies in the countryside, practising agriculture and controlling the routes through the valleys.

CORTONA itself only appears to have become a city in the 4th century (the 3rd-century walls and the Academy Museum are open to the public) and only begins to figure in Etruscan history quite late—in the war against Rome in 310 B.C.

By the end of the 6th century the major centre of the area was

63

64

65

63. Arezzo, Roman amphiteatre (1st century A.D.).

64-65. Two examples of "Aretini" vases (1st century B.C.–1st century A.D.). Arezzo, Archaeological Museum.

AREZZO. Among the earliest evidence are the first city walls (some parts are still intact), a necropolis of ditch tombs (Poggio al Sole), and some sanctuaries documented either by architectural terracottas (such as the slab from Piazza San Jacopo, now in the Archaeological Museum) or by votive offerings such as the one from Fonte Veneziana consisting of small bronze male and female figures (Archaeological Museum, Florence; other similar ones in Arezzo). In the 4th century Arezzo witnessed rebellions by the serfs: the first one, around the middle of the century, was quelled by Aulus Spurinna; the second, in 302, by the Roman army. During this period (4th-3rd century) the prosperity of the city is documented by a few, but remarkable, buildings, such as the masonry walls (partly still standing); among the artifacts dating from this period are many coins and the famous bronze statue of the Chimaera, probably produced in Arezzo where there were metallurgical workshops. Among the objects dating from the 2nd century are the Hellenistic style terracottas found at Catona (Archaeological Museum, Florence) and at the sanctuary of Castelsecco, near the city, which consisted of many buildings, including a small theatre.

There is very little evidence from the Villanovan and archaic Oriental periods in the territory of FIESOLE apart from some fragments of pottery in the museum in Fiesole and a few finds in the centre of Florence. In the 7th-6th centuries the most characteristic aspect of this area are the grand tombs, like the two *tholoi* at Quinto Fiorentino (Montagnola and Mula, both open to the public), the tumulus of Montefortini and the tomb of the Boschetti at Comeana (near Artimino; some of the objects are in the Antiquarium of the Medici villa), containing artifacts in gold and ivory, mostly produced in southern Etruria. These are the tombs of the local nobility who controlled the road to Marzabotto and Bologna along the valley of the Reno. Until quite late the population lived in scattered settlements, if we are to believe the evidence offered by the typical

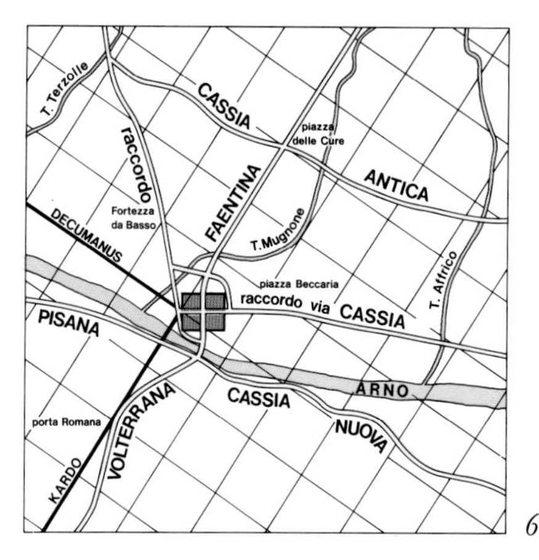

66. Fiesole, Roman theatre (1st century A.D.).

67. Fiesole, ruins of the Roman baths (1st century A.D.).

68. The Roman city of Florence, with the surrounding division into "centuries" and the Roman roads.

local stone funerary steles decorated in Ionic style with warriors or with banquet and dance scenes (museums in Florence and Fiesole) and the little bronzes from the small sanctuaries of the area (excellent examples in the local museum).

Fiesole became an urban community in the Hellenistic period, when the walls (3rd century, in part still standing) and a temple consisting of a cella and *alae* were built.

As early as 302 B.C, the revolt of the serfs in AREZZO against the most powerful local family, the *Cilnii* (the ancestors of Maecenas), led to the intervention of the Roman consul Valerius Maximus. During the 3rd century Arezzo became part of Rome's network of alliances, but the city retained a great productive capacity and contributed an enormous number of bronze weapons towards Scipio's campaign in Africa in 205 B.C.—a sure sign of its economic prosperity. At the time of Sulla the city became a colony: the new inhabitants were called *Fidentiores* to distinguish them from the old ones, *Arretini veteres*. Later, at the time of Caesar, more colonizers settled here: they were called *Iulienses*. With the increase of population, Arezzo spread outside the city walls; the most recent set of walls, dating from the 4th-3rd century, was built in half-baked bricks. Another element that favoured Arezzo's prosperity was the construction of the Cassian Way (before 217 B.C.) connecting the city to Rome and the rest of inland northern Etruria.

By the middle of the 1st century B.C. there were many ceramics industries producing fine tableware: terracotta, plates, goblets and glasses, covered by a thick layer of coral-red glossy paint. These vases, called "aretini," were extremely sought after and reached even the furthest outposts of the Roman empire. This industry continued to prosper until the middle of the 1st century A.D. when many other Italian centres started producing similar wares and the competition of other provincial manufacturers contributed to its decline.

Religion and Divination

As early as the Middle Palaeolithic, funeral rites presuppose a continuation of life after death (tools and food offerings in the tombs). The objects found in tombs dating from the Upper Palaeolithic prove that there must have been a belief in a very complex spiritual world, about which we know little.

The Neolithic agricultural economy was tied to fertility rites and cults of the changing seasons; evidence of these lies in the holes in grottoes containing offerings, which also may be connected to funeral rites and spirits of the underworld, and in stone circles with human remains, vases and other precious objects. There is also evidence of the worship of water deities. Similar rites continued throughout the metal ages, and in some cases the same site was used continually from the Neolithic to classical times. Megalithic monuments and stele statues, found in Europe and in the western Mediterranean region, are evidence of even more complex cults.

According to the Roman historian Livy, the Etruscans were a people particularly given over to religious worship, for they excelled in its practice. Latin writers, such as Cicero and Seneca, recall that the Etruscans used a series of written doctrines, both religious and civil (*Libri fulgurales, haruspicini, rituales*). The revelation of these texts was ascribed to the boy Tages, miraculously born out of a furrow in the countryside near Tarquinia. The foundation of all doctrine (in Latin, *disciplina*) was the division of the heavens into sixteen regions, the dwellings of the gods; to the east the favourable ones, to the west the unfavourable. This division, based on the two axes east-west and north-south, determined the allocation of any space that was to be used for either sacred or civil practices, starting from the cities, which were founded along the two axes. This system of division was used everywhere, down to the animal liver which was the most common, but not the only, instrument used for divining, or interpreting the will of the gods. We know of this from several figurative representations and from the small bronze model of a liver (late 2nd century B.C.) now in Piacenza. The outer part is divided into sixteen parts, and each one is inscribed with the name of a god. The science of divination was practised exclusively by the *haruspices* (in Etruscan, *netsvis*), who formed an aristocratic caste and wore special clothing. They were honoured and respected even in Rome, from the 4th century B.C. until the late classical period.

The *Etrusca disciplina* was the aspect of religion in which the Romans felt most strongly the influence of the Etruscans. It is thanks to the fact that the

I

II

III

Romans adopted this ritual that it has come down to us. According to Varro, the ritual surrounding the foundation of Rome was based on the ritual of the foundation of Etruscan cities. And during the Punic wars Rome made use of *haruspices* brought in from Etruria (in fact there were no *haruspices* among the Roman high priests). During the 2nd century B.C., perhaps after the discovery of impostors, the Roman Senate decreed that there should be a fixed number of people authorized to practise divination: it is possibly at this time that the college of the sixty *haruspices* was instituted in Tarquinia. Under Emperor Claudius the discipline of divination was included among the branches of the official Roman religion.

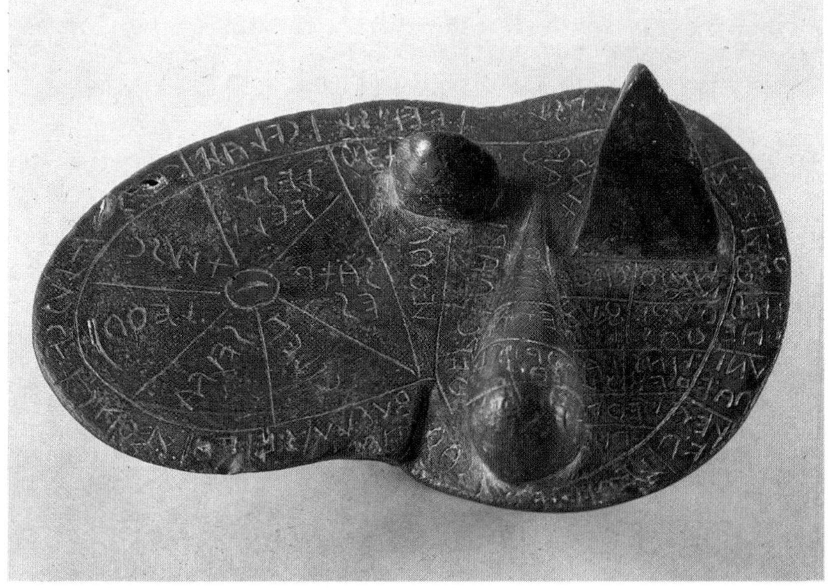

IV

I. Reconstruction of a divination ceremony. The drawing, elaborating ancient portrayals, reconstructs a scene in which the haruspex, *in a ritual pose and with special clothing, interprets an animal liver before an attentive audience, conscious of the solemnity of the ceremony.*

II. The urn of Aule Lecu (early 1st century B.C.). Volterra, Guarnacci Museum. The deceased is portrayed as an haruspex, *reading the omens of an animal liver.*

III. Reverse side of a bronze mirror showing the mythical seer Calchas dressed as an haruspex *examining an animal liver (from Vulci, early 4th century B.C.). Vatican, Gregorian Etruscan Museum.*

IV. Bronze model of a sheep's liver (from Decima di Gossolengo, late 2nd–early 1st century B.C.). Piacenza, Civic Museum. Names of deities are inscribed in the different shaped subdivisions.

69

70

71

69. Gold thread used for brocade (from Arezzo, first half of the 7th century). Florence, Archaeological Museum.

70. Gold pendant earrings (from Arezzo, first half of the 7th century). Florence, Archaeological Museum.

72

The trademarks stamped on these vases provide us with useful information about the characteristics of this industry.

There are many important remains of the Roman Arezzo. The basic plan of the town appears to date from the time of Caesar. An exact copy of the *Elogia* in the Forum of Augustus in Rome has been found in the forum, near the cathedral. Ruins of the amphitheatre and of the foundations of the theatre are visible. The Archaeological Museum stands on the site of the amphitheatre and houses a marvellous collection of "aretini" vases.

In the course of the 2nd century A.D. the city suffered a pronounced decline, partly a result of the waning ceramics industry and partly because the Cassian Way had been moved further away from the city centre.

During the civil war, FIESOLE sided with Marius; at the end of the war, the victorious Sulla reacted by founding a colony there. A fire, probably at the time of the civil war, destroyed the Etruscan temple which was reconstructed at the time of Sulla with the addition of a portico with columns and steps. A road connects the temple and the theatre, which was partly dug out of the hillside; nearby there are baths built at the time of Augustus. The local museum houses a good collection of Roman materials. The development of Florence in the 1st century A.D. led to Fiesole's rapid decline.

When, at the time of Caesar, FLORENCE (*Florentia*) became a Roman colony, it was given a regular plan, built around *cardines* (streets running north-south) and *decumani* (streets running east-west). The intersection of these streets gave rise to blocks of varying sizes. Archaeological research has shown that the forum must have been at the centre of the city; several public buildings were built along its sides, such as the *Capitolium*. Some areas within the walls remained for a long time without buildings but, by the 1st century A.D., the town had spread even outside the walls, especially to the south, towards the Arno. At the same time, many new public buildings were built: baths in the area behind the *Capitolium*, and a theatre. It seems that to build the theatre part of the walls had to be demolished.

73

74

Like other towns of northern Etruria—but in contrast to those further south—it seems that Florence survived as a city until quite late. During the 2nd century the forum was enlarged and paved with marble slabs; new baths, a temple to Isis and an amphitheatre were built outside the walls. Still fairly prosperous in the 3rd and 4th centuries, Florence underwent further transformations and became the capital of *Tuscia et Umbria* at the time of Diocletian (297 A.D.). By the 4th century the city had spread to the north as far as Piazza San Lorenzo, where, at the end of the century, St Ambrose consecrated a Christian basilica. To the south, the city had reached the Arno.

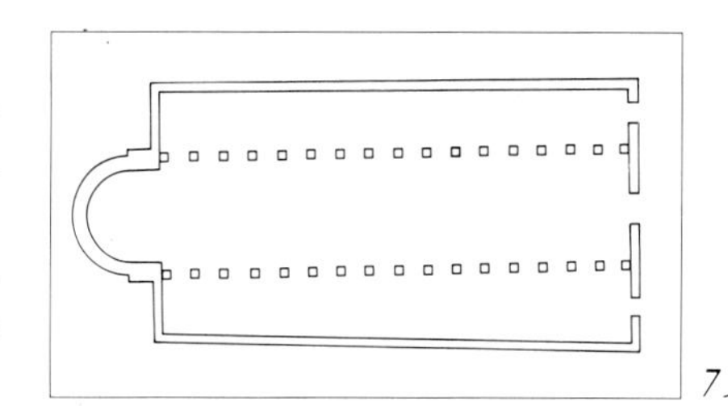

75

76

At the time of the Longobards, the diocese of AREZZO ruled over an enormous area, from the Casentino to Cortona and from Montevarchi to the river Arbia, but we have so little information that we are unable to reconstruct either the events of the first three centuries of the early Middle Ages or the characteristics of the region, except along very general lines. The most valuable element available to modern researchers is the network of churches, which, however, have no fragments of sculpture dating from the first phase of Longobard domination. There are some materials from the Longobard period in the Medieval and Modern Museum in Arezzo: among these, a *sax* (sort of long knife) and two *spathae* (swords) which an X-ray examination have revealed to be damascened. But the most interesting materials come from the excavations on the site of the old cathedral, on the Pionta hill (razed to the ground by the Medici in 1561): in the tomb of a small girl there were, as well as the gold thread from the brocade veil, a pair of gold earrings with pendants with regular settings—green glass paste and amethyst drops—in a late Roman style very popular among the Byzantines and adopted also by the Longobards (first half of the 7th century; there are other examples in the Archaeological Museum of Grosseto and in that of Florence, found at Santa Cristina near Bolsena).

Among the few examples of early medieval architecture in Tuscany, the only one that seems to have kept its original characteristics is the little temple of Santo Stefano in the plain of ANGHIARI. Today it is in the diocese of Arezzo, but it was originally in that of Città di Castello, a city that probably grew up around a Byzantine fortification and later developed into a Longobard outpost. The building is square in plan, built in bricks and decorated with blind arches outside. Inside, the nave and two aisles are divided by round arches, resting on columns, and a vestibule. The church, which probably dates from the 7th century, is connected to the civilization of Ravenna. It has also been suggested that it represents the theological symbol of the Trinity, in an area which was for a long time Arian.

In the war between the Greeks and the Goths, FLORENCE was a Byzantine stronghold and was besieged by Totila. During the Longobard occupation, together with eastern Tuscany, Florence was part of a region whose main centres were Lucca and the new Via Francigena, for neighbouring Romagna was still dom-

71. Gold earrings (from Santa Cristina near Bolsena, first half of the 7th century). Florence, Archaeological Museum.

72. Anghiari, temple of Santo Stefano (7th century).

73. Florence, the apse of the church of Santa Reparata.

74. Florence, fragments of the mosaic floor of the original church of Santa Reparata (6th century).

75. Ground-plan of the early Christian church of Santa Reparata.

76. Ground-plan of the pre-Romanesque and Romanesque church of Santa Reparata.

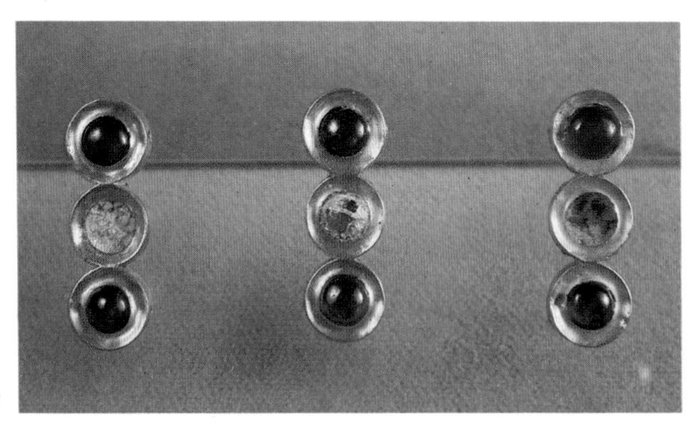

77

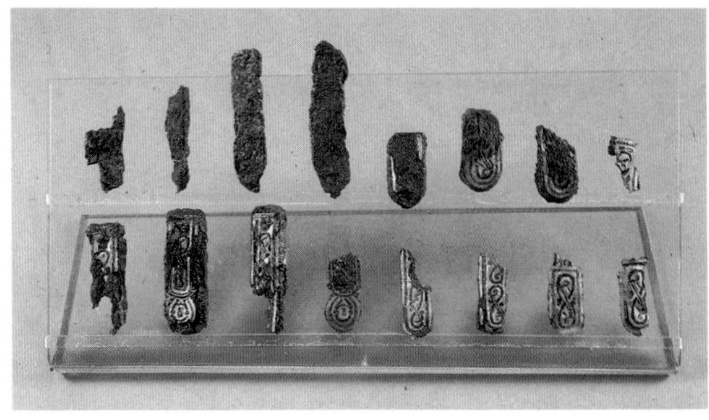

78

79

77. Necklace clasps (from tomb 21 at Fiesole, 7th-8th century). Fiesole, Archaeological Museum.

78. Fragments of damascened belt decorations (7th-8th century). Fiesole, Archaeological Museum.

79. The development of the city of Florence up to the early Middle Ages.
Red: the Roman city (59 B.C.).
Red dotted line: the maximum expansion during the Roman period (2nd century A.D.; around 10,000 inhabitants).
Green: the Byzantine *castrum* (541-568; around 1,000 inhabitants).
Purple: the Carolingian walls (late 9th century; around 5,000 inhabitants).
Yellow: the walls built by Countess Matilde (1078; around 20,000 inhabitants).
I. The river Mugnone during the Roman period.
II. The river Mugnone after its course was changed in 1078 – today's Via Tornabuoni.

inated by the Byzantines. Under the Franks, the city became the seat of a county; under the Ottonians, it became part of the marquisate of Tuscany. Florence, with its Roman origins, had a unique relationship with Fiesole, of Etruscan origin: both were the seats of dioceses, but their territories were more or less interwoven. It was only in 1125 that Florence definitively asserted its hegemony, destroying what little autonomy Fiesole had left.

The excavation of Santa Reparata, under the cathedral of Florence, has provided us with a wealth of materials documenting the history of the city in the Middle Ages, especially between the 4th and 11th centuries. The Roman occupation came to an end at the beginning of the 5th century, when the city was conquered by Radagaisus in 406. The church of Santa Reparata was founded around the year 500. Even in its name it is evidence of very close ties with the religion practised in Ravenna and the Exarchate. Ten panels of the floor mosaic have survived: they are decorated with quatrefoils, with facing lozenges and peltas, surrounded by swastikas, circles and meanders with peacocks in the middle. It is so similar to decorations from the region along the northern Adriatic, that it enables us to date it at the 6th century. We know that the church was in use during the 7th century thanks to the objects found in a Longobard tomb. A second phase, "Carolingian" (9th century), witnessed the construction of a crypt and the addition of two trapeze-shaped turrets, forming almost a transept. It was probably at this time that the seat of the bishopric was transferred from San Lorenzo to Santa Reparata by Bishop Andrea. The body of the founding bishop, Saint Zenobius, was also moved to the site which, until 1965, was called the "mortuary chapel of Saint Zenobius" and constituted the only trace in Santa Maria del Fiore of the earlier cathedral. A third phase, Romanesque, dates from the time of Bishop Gerardo (mid-11th century), who came from Burgundy. This phase il closely connected to Cluniac architecture. The church was completely reconstructed, and the side chapels and small apses were added as well as pilasters with transversal arches at the crossing and a rough marble and stone pavement. The style was basically "retrospective", indicating solidarity with Cluny, as opposed to "progressive", like the cathedral of Pisa built soon afterwards.

The Archaeological Museum in FIESOLE houses several early medieval objects from Longobard necropolises around the theatre, in Piazza Mino da Fiesole and villa Marchi, as well as some pottery found in a well in Piazza Mino (10th-11th century). We know neither the size nor the exact location of the early medieval settlement, although it must have been nearby and certainly within the Etruscan walls. The tombs, dating from the late 6th and 7th centuries, are built of upright stones, covered in stone slabs: the reconstruction of one such tomb is visible at the entrance to the excavations. The pottery found in them consisted mostly of objects produced locally, but there were also some imported pieces, such as an African bowl or a set of bottles very similar to those produced in the area of the lower Rhein valley. A particularly interesting collection of personal objects belonging to a woman includes fragments of gold brocade and necklace clasps. Among the men's personal objects there were spearheads, *spathae* (swords) and bejewelled belt buckles and decorations, a technique typical of Longobard craftsmanship in Italy. The pottery from the well in Piazza Mino, mostly table and kitchen goblets, were found in 1879 together with some wooden buckets, on view in the same room of the museum. One of these, examined with C14, has enabled us to date the objects at the 10th-11th century.

PISA, LUCCA AND LUNI

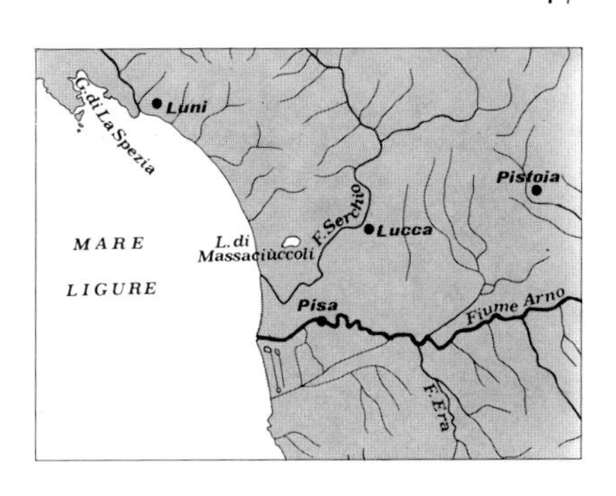

The Lower Palaeolithic is represented by shards found at Livorno, by bifacial implements around Livorno and in the lower Arno valley. Numerous surface finds from the Mousterian period are in the area around Livorno, at Massaciuccoli and in caves of the Apuan Alps. The Upper Palaeolithic is well documented in almost all its aspects in the area around Livorno, at Massaciuccoli, in the lower valley of the Arno and in the Lima valley. Microlithic mesolithic finds come from the passes on the Appennines. The Neolithic period is documented by impressed ceramics found near Pisa, particularly at the Riparo La Romita at Asciano, which has provided us with objects from the Neolithic—represented by incised line pottery and the cultures of Lagozza and Diana—through to the barbarian invasions. On the sand dunes near San Rossore we have found evidence of a settlement characterized by incised line pottery and late Lagozza culture objects; other Lagozza culture remains were found at Grotta dell'Onda and at Massaciuccoli. The documentation of the Neolithic is also abundant: there are finds from its early stage (Romita, Grotta del Leone, Grotta dell'Onda, San Rossore) and from later periods, characterized by the local influences of the Rinaldone culture and other northern trends, represented only by tombs in crevices and caves in the mountainous areas (Monte Pisano, Apuan Alps, Garfagnana, Lunigiana). There are also elements from the bell-shaped vase culture. The Bronze Age is less well represented, with just a few fragments at Romita, some non-representative finds at Coltano and occasional fragments found in the proto-Villanovan grottoes and shelters at Gabbro, Limone and Pariana. Also worthy of mention, in Lunigiana, are the stele-statues dating from all the various metal ages. (Materials are in the Archeological Museum in Florence, in the Florentine Prehistorical Museum, at the Faculty of Anthropology at Pisa, at the Civic Museum in Viareggio, at Villa Guinigi in Lucca, at the Archaeological Museum at Casola in Lunigiana and at the Malaspina Castle at Pontremoli).

The territory of PISA consisted in the stretch of the Arno valley from San Miniato to the sea and the coastal area from Castiglioncello to Serravezza in archaic times, to Camaiore from the middle of the 3rd century B.C. onwards. Like the territory of Fiesole, it was a typical border region, as is proved also by the variability of its northern frontier. The stretch along the coast was dotted with small settlements from the end of the 7th century onwards; these communities prospered thanks to maritime trade. Among them were Massarosa and the town documented by the warehouse discovered in Piazza dei Cavalieri in Pisa, where the large number of amphoras is evidence of the importance of this commercial port used by Phocaean merchants. From the 5th century, the connections between the territory of Pisa and the towns on the other side of the Appennines is documented by ceramics, small bronze statues and typical pear-shaped marble inscribed stones resting on square bases decorated with rams' heads which will soon be on view in the new Museo dell'Opera della Primaziale in Pisa. These finds show the ties between Pisa and Volterra (there are similar objects in the Guarnacci Museum in Volterra) and Marzabotto and Sasso Marconi. The communication route—along the valley of the Arno, the Serchio and the Enza—is documented by many finds, such as the tombs in the Bien-

80

8

80. Lagozza culture ceramics from Grotta del Leone, Agnano, Neolithic). Pisa, Institute of Anthropology.

81. Stele-statues from Lunigiana (metal ages). La Spezia, Civic Museum.

tina basin (at that time crossed by the river *Auser*, today called Serchio) with their Attic gold jewellery and pottery, and the necropolis of Ponte a Moriano (first half of the 3rd century) with its many references to the aristocratic family *Percna*, also found at Spina (see the items now in Villa Guinigi in Lucca).

We know very little of the development of Pisa. From around the middle of the 3rd century B.C., it became a Roman stronghold against the Gauls and the Ligurians, who were beginning to move southward, and against Hannibal. The strong presence of the Roman army in the area led to the foundation of Lucca in the territory of Pisa (180 B.C.) and of Luni in Ligurian territory (177 B.C.). The prosperity of the area at the time is documented by a few finds in Pisa, by the tombs of Fonte Vivo (on the site of the town hall of San Miniato) and by the pre-Roman ruins under the baptistry of Lucca. Here, as well as the *kelebai* (black ceramics of Volterran origin), archaeologists have also found imported objects. Particularly worthy of mention are two female statues in marble (end of the 3rd century), one from Pisa (new Museo dell'Opera della Primaziale) and the other from San Miniato (Archaeological Museum in Florence), comparable to the Volterran sculpture of the time. After the foundation of Luni, it appears that Pisa lost importance as a port, while the small port of Castiglioncello developed and flourished for the whole of the 2nd century (tombs in the Archaeological Museum in Florence).

Is was only under Augustus that LUCCA was included in the region of Etruria and its territory was divided into "centuries." Lucca had previously been a fairly important centre because of its position along the communication routes, and it remained one under the Romans. In 56 B.C. it was in Lucca that Caesar, Pompey and Crassus met to renew their agreement (First Triumvirate).

The city was surrounded by walls (some parts are still visible at

82

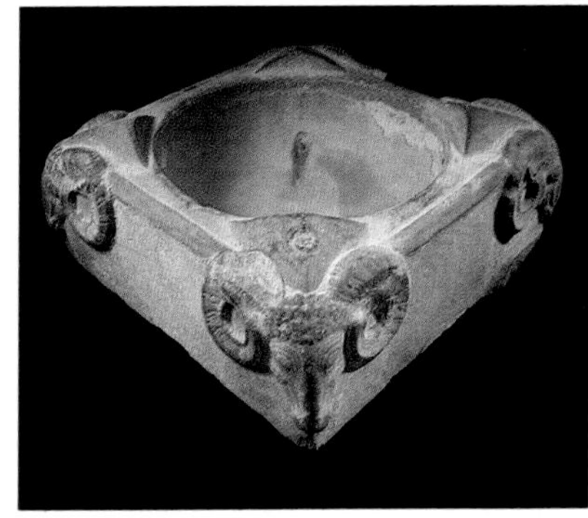

83

82. Lucca, ruins of the Roman walls in the church of Santa Maria della Rosa.

83. Base of a marble cippus, decorated with rams' heads (from the area around Pisa, early 5th century B.C.). Pisa, Museo dell'Opera della Primaziale.

Santa Maria della Rosa) and laid out according to a regular plan rather like those of military camps (*castra*). During the late imperial age, the walls were provided with watchtowers. Within the walls there was a theatre (ruins near Sant'Agostino), while outside there was an amphitheatre, later incorporated into some medieval buildings that maintained, however, its circular shape. The area of the arena is today the Piazza del Mercato. Objects found in Lucca and surroundings are in the Villa Guinigi Museum.

The port of LUNI (*Luna* was the pre-Roman name) overlooks the gulf of La Spezia. It must have been important, active and accessible to the Romans even before the founding of the colony (177 B.C.). It was from here that Consul Cato set off towards Spain in 194 B.C. The town, on the left bank of the Magra, became part of Etruria and marked its northern boundary. It was probably at the time of the founding of the colony that the town was given its regular plan, with the usual grid of streets intersecting at right angles. The area where the forum was built must have been a public space even before; two temples, dating from the very first years of the colony, stood there (the architectural terracottas which decorated them are in the Archaeological Museum in Florence). On a slightly higher level and facing in a different direction, there was the *Capitolium*) a tripartite temple dedicated to Jupiter, Juno and Minerva) built later than the first two temples. The *Via Aemilia Scauri* separates the *Capitolium* from the forum. At that stage it was the continuation of the Via Aurelia, and will be called that after the 3rd century A.D. In recent years, systematic excavations have taken place in Luni, bringing to light many buildings including some private houses, many of which are very large and have mosaic floors. The walls were built partly in concrete, partly in large blocks of local stone. Both Rutilius Namatianus at the beginning of the 5th century A.D. and Ciriaco of Ancona in the 15th mentioned the existence of marble walls, but they probably mistook the ruins of some other building for the city

Agriculture and the Agrarian landscape

The earliest agricultural activity is documented by palaeobotanical remains (wheat, barley, millet, beans, lentils) and by agricultural tools: fragments of sickles, grindstones and stone mullers, wells and underground silos for the preservation of foodstuffs.

The appropriation of land and the subsequent setting up of borders lies at the root of the development of the Etruscan people: the boundaries of the land are considered sacred, they are the projection of a cosmic order based on the separation of the elements, as is shown by the prophecy of Vegoia and by the numerous inscribed stones marking property divisions (see p. 31). In agriculture, contact with the Greek world introduced several more rational innovations: the practice of fallowing (the alternation of leguminous crops and wheat crops), the cultivation of the vine (7th century) and of the olive (5th century), and even the instrument used for measuring the land, the *groma*, for which even the name was borrowed from the Greek. Classical writers tell us how remarkably fertile the Etruscan fields were, so much so that the Roman populace, after the fall of Veii, wanted to move to the newly conquered territory because it was more fertile (Livy). But we also know that all this fertility was due to man's intervention as well. This intensive agricultural activity did not decline even when Etruria lost its independence, for all the Etruscan cities, except Arezzo and Populonia, supplied Scipio's African campaign (205 B.C.) with agricultural produce and timber.

The agrarian landscape of Etruria in Roman times is strictly connected to the territory's political and administrative set-up. On the land controlled by the allied cities the traditional Etruscan cultivation methods continued to predominate, whereas in those areas where the Roman presence was more direct, such as the colonies, the landscape began to look more like that of Latium and Campania. The land was divided anto centuries (a system of measuring and dividing the land according to the intersection of axes at right angles) and the plots granted to the colonizing farmers. The colonizers lived in the city if their property was nearby, or in farms on the land. The fields surrounding these modest dwellings, usually housing only one family, were used for mixed crops. The vine, for example, was "married" to supporting trees and the rest of the field was taken up by grain, vegetables and leguminous plants, and whatever else might be necessary for the survival of the family. Often, however, the produce of the land was not sufficient and then portions of public land (*ager pubblicus*) were taken over, primarily as pasture land. When the high-ranking citizens of Rome, mostly members of the Senate, began to appropriate the land, setting up large landed estates controlled by villas, the agricultural activity became more spe-

I

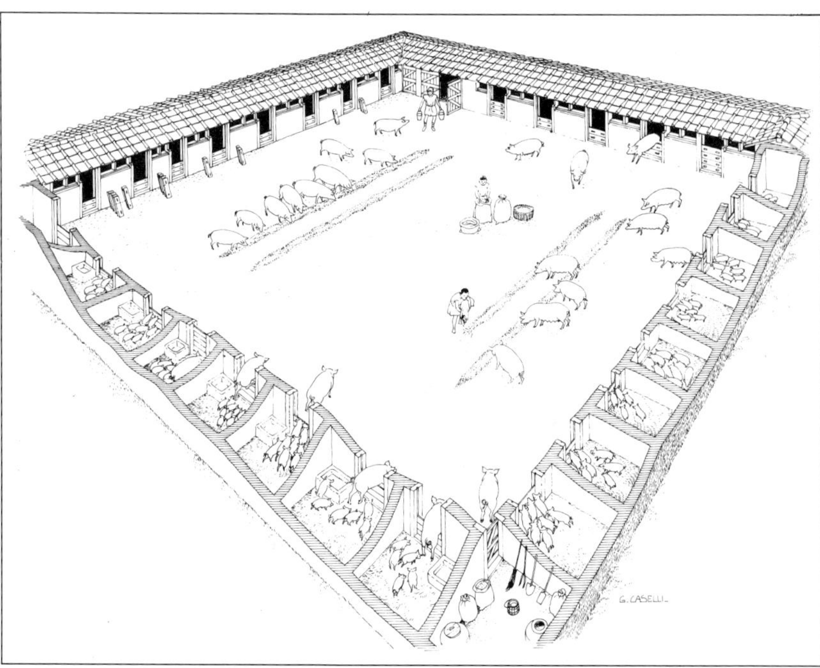

II

cialized and intensive. The crops were mostly exported. For the most part the cultivations consisted in vines, olives, fruit trees, leguminous plants and grain (in rotation on the same fields) and anything else that was necessary to feed the numerous agricultural labourers that lived in the villa. The majority of these workers were slaves. During the middle and late imperial age the land became progressively more the property of the emperor, and the appearance of the landscape changed considerably. Intensive cultivation was replaced by extensive (the alternation of wheat, fallow and pasture). The villas were replaced, starting in the 2nd century A.D., by a few very large buildings (among which the maritime villas) connected to the development of these vast and underpopulated estates.

The peasants and farmers were probably the ones who were less affected by the fall of the Roman empire and the impact with the Germanic tribes, for the Longobards adopted the Roman laws governing land division. The system of the *curtis*, which in Tuscany is documented primarily through the large ecclesiastical estates, was organized rather loosely around the *curtis* itself, the direct descendant of the late Roman villa. Large estates might consist of more than one *curtis*, even quite far apart from each other. Division and subdivision were the fundamental characteristics of early medieval agrarian landscape, both because of mixed cultivations and for the very nature of the *curtis*, within which the property was divided into *sorti*, *mansi* and *petia de terra*. Some of these had a house on them where freed men or serfs lived, while the overlord's part, controlled directly, consisted also of pasture land and woods. During the early Middle Ages many changes took place in the distribution of settlements and population: the initial preponderance of scattered settlements in the plains was replaced progressively by hilltop communities.

I. The so-called "Ponte Sodo" at Veii (5th century B.C.). Actually, it is an artificial tunnel which was used to change the course of the Cremera river.

II. Reconstruction of the large pigsty in the Roman villa at Settefinestre near Cosa.

III. Small bronze votive statue of a man ploughing (from Arezzo, late 5th century B.C.). Rome, Villa Giulia.

IV. Relief showing slaves pressing grapes. Aquileia, Archaeological Museum.

III

IV

84

84. Lucca, the arcades of the Roman amphitheatre.

85

85. Lucca, aerial view; in the lower part, the market square built on the site of the Roman Amphitheatre.

walls. Outside the walls, the ruins of the amphitheatre are still visible, and, within the walls, there was a theatre built in the Julian-Claudian period. The relatively small size of this theatre makes one suppose that the population was quite small. An event which added to the prosperity of the town must have been the discovery of the quarries of white marble, called Lunensian or Carrara marble, which was used for the first time, according to Pliny, in 48 B.C. Between 40 and 30 B.C. its usage became widespread and, by the time of Augustus, it was used in large quantities in Rome and the provinces. The blocks of marble were transported by sea to the mouth of the Tiber, then carried to the various parts of the capital. The town of Luni must also have prospered thanks to the surrounding fertile plain. Both Pliny and Martial speak of the famous large cheeses and Pliny thought that the wine from Luni was the best in Etruria. The amphoras used for transporting wine are evidence of a thriving wine trade as early as the 1st century B.C.

Of Roman PISA, on the other hand, we know very little. There are inscriptions which document its importance, among which the *Elogia pisana*, recording the honours tributed to Caius and Lucius Caesari (2-4 A.D.), which can be seen together with other Roman items at the Camposanto. The location of the various buildings in the city is still not known (there are remains of baths, known as "Nero's baths," near Porta a Lucca). Many pieces of Roman marble (mostly from Rome and Ostia) were reused in the construction of later important buildings, such as the cathedral. Many Roman sarcophagi were also reused between the 11th and 15th centuries; they may be seen at the Camposanto.

We know very little about early medieval LUCCA, despite the fact that it was the capital of the region; it was occupied by the Longobards very early—probably before 570—and they settled within the Roman walls, as is documented by the finds at Santa Giulia and San Romano, later spreading out to the countryside as well (see, for example, the burial site at Marlia). Among the Longobard objects

86

87

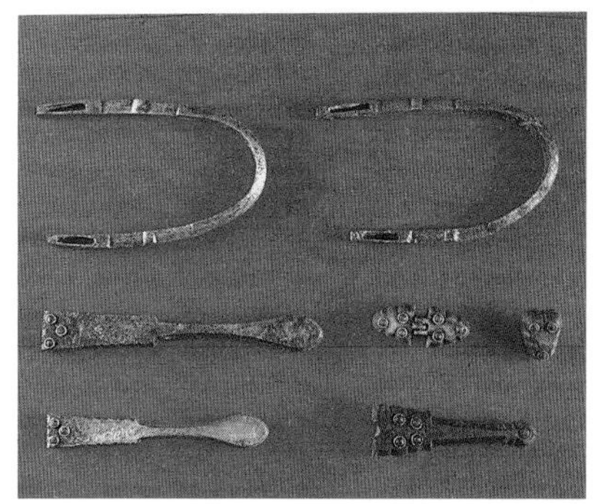

88

86. Luni, aerial view of the Roman amphitheatre.

87. Bronze laminas belonging to a parade shield (from San Romano, second half of the 7th century). Lucca, Villa Guinigi.

88. Bronze spurs, spearheads, plaque and studs (from San Romano, second half of the 7th century). Lucca, Villa Guinigi.

found in the tombs are the little gold crosses, sometimes decorated with geometric or animal patterns (in relief or engraved), which were sewn onto the cloth covering the face of the deceased. For a long time it was believed that this custom was solely Germanic, but more recent studies have proved that it is Italic or Mediterranean in origin. Five gold leaf crosses were found in more than one tomb at Santa Giulia, where the very elaborate gold apparel of a knight was also discovered. All these objects are now in the museum at Villa Guinigi together with parts of a parade shield found at San Romano (7th century): the *umbo*, the central part of the shield, and the metal plates that decorated the wooden part, showing Archangel Michael, protector of the Longobards, or Daniel in the lion's den, or even the deceased himself.

Longobard presence in the area is also documented by the finds at Piazza del Serchio and San Lorenzo a Vaccoli (where the Longobards first settled and began their conquest of Tuscany), by the famous "Lamina" of Agilulf (a gold leaf pectoral ornament), found in the Valdinievole area (now in the Bargello National Museum of Florence) and, above all, by the discoveries in Piazza dei Miracoli in Pisa, where there was a necropolis laid out on Roman foundations. Here, belts with precious stone decorations were found; the patterns consist of entwined snakelike animals (second half of the 7th century, Museo di San Matteo in Pisa) that are comparable to north Tyrolean belts of the same period.

The decline of the cities and of the urban organization is particularly evident as early as the 6th century at LUNI, where a systematic archaeological dig, begun only a few years ago, has brought to light two extremely poor houses in the area that had been the forum. They show holes where the poles stood and stones from earlier constructions have been used. They are evidence of an obviously widespread lifestyle that archaeologists, however, still know little about, except that it must have existed even before the arrival of the Germanic tribes.

The Longobard presence is documented by the bronze objects from tombs (burial by inhumation), frequently even within the city walls: fibulas, buckles, armillas and brooches, all more or less in the Byzantine tradition but quite similar to objects found in the Longobard necropolises at Castelvecchio (Verona), Testona (Turin), Santa Giulia (Lucca) and so on.

After an interruption of almost a century, archaeologists have recently resumed work on the basilica of Luni. The construction was formally a cathedral from the middle of the 9th century until 1204, when the seat of the diocese was transferred to Sarzana. The basilica was built in at least three different stages and its foundations are Roman.

VOLTERRA, POPULONIA AND SIENA

The Lower Palaeolithic is represented by shards found at Bibbona and by a bifacial implement from Monastero d'Ombrone; the Middle Palaeolithic by surface finds along the valleys of the Merse and the Farma. The archaic Upper Palaeolithic is documented at Montalcino and the Gravettian at Monte San Savino. An incised shard, showing a bison, was found at Lustignano. The Neolithic is represented only by a few fragments of impressed pottery found at Piombino, while the Aeneolithic is documented by the ditch tombs at Pomarance, Guardistallo, Camigliano and Monteroni d'Arbia, by the Grotta di Sant'Antimo near Montalcino and by the little grotto tomb at Montebradoni near Volterra. The Bronze Age is represented by the collections of early objects found at Campiglia, Castiglion d'Orcia, Sovicille and Populonia, and by various other single finds. (Objects in the Pigorini Museum in Rome and in the Archaeological Museums of Siena and Florence).

Materials dating from the Villanovan culture (9th-7th centuries B.C.) have been found near VOLTERRA, in the necropolises of Badia, Ripaie and Guerruccia; they show close connections with the civilization of Bologna at the time (see the objects in the Guarnacci Museum in Volterra). The "Oriental" phase was less developed here: it was still tied to the Villanovan tradition, as far as funeral ritual was concerned, although it also shows some analogies with contemporary southern Etrurian civilizations. Particularly interesting are the cinerary urn of Montescudaio (mid-7th century) which has on its lid, executed in an elementary sculptural form, a representation of the deceased at a banquet; the bucchero *kyathos* from Monteriggioni, imported from southern Etruria (examples in the Guarnacci Museum); the q [1] tomb from Badia (about 650-625 B.C.) on view in the museum, which contained Etruscan-Corinthian oil jars proving that Volterra had commercial ties with southern Etruria, via the port of Populonia. From the early 6th century onwards, the typical *tholos* tombs began to be used throughout the area: they are formed by rows of stone slabs, each row projecting further than the previous one, sustained by a central pilaster. All these *tholoi*, or beehive tombs, were found in the valley of the Cecina, at Casale Marittimo (reconstructed in the Archaeological Museum in Florence), at Casaglia (reconstructed in the garden of the town hall of Cecina), at Bolgheri and at Bibbona (no longer standing). The objects in them (Archaeological Museum, Florence), mostly imported from southern Etruria, are analogous to the contemporary ones from Populonia, which in the archaic period was the area's only port. Some sources even state that Populonia was founded by Volterra. It is likely that it is also thanks to the ties with Populonia that a casket full of Phocaean and Massalian coins (Archaeological Museum, Florence) arrived in Volterra and that the artistic activities of the second half of the 6th century were characterized by a "Ionic" style: inscribed steles with figures of knights (examples in the museum), some bronze statuettes and the so-called "Lorenzini head" (about 480 B.C.), in marble, probably belonging to the full-figure statue of a god.

It was at this time, thanks particularly to the copper mining in the area, that the city as such was born; the walls were built (no

89

90

89. Reconstruction of the tholos tomb of Casale Marittimo (around 620-600 B.C.). Florence, Archaeological Museum.

90. Stone funerary stele, with dedicatory inscription to Avile Tite, portrayed as a warrior (550-525 B.C.). Volterra, Guarnacci Museum.

longer standing) as well as stone buildings with tiled roofs on the Acropolis. The marble bases of inscribed stones, decorated with rams' heads, and the recurrence of the name *Kaikna* on three steles in Bologna are evidence of Volterra's participation in the refounding of Felsina (Bologna) and the foundation of Marzabotto (early 5th century).

From the 4th century to the end of the 2nd, Volterra experienced its period of greatest prosperity, probably thanks to its well-organized plan of intensive agriculture which we have discovered through the presence of several small settlements scattered throughout the countryside. By this time Volterra ruled over a vast territory: the stretch of coast from the river Fine to Bolgheri, the valleys of the Cecina and of the Era, the valley of the Elsa and the fortress of Monteriggioni. The city built a new set of enormous walls (which are still standing in some places, such as Badia), began to coin money and to produce a typical kind of ceramic ware (red-figure kraters and ceramic varnished black and then painted; examples in the Guarnacci Museum). This pottery was exported, throughout the 4th, 3rd and 2nd centuries, to the towns of northern Etruria, of Liguria, beyond the Appennines as far as Adria and Spina and even to

91

92

91. Reconstruction of the Inghirami tomb at Volterra (2nd century B.C.). Florence, Archaeological Museum.

Corsica (Aleria). Particularly important is the collection of cinerary urns (Archaeological Museum in Florence and Guarnacci Museum in Volterra) which follow, at a remarkably high artistic level, the various currents of the Hellenistic period (Microasiatic, Rhodic, Pergamonic, Classicistic). The Hellenistic style is also evident in the architectural terracottas found in the temple on the Acropolis, which was rebuilt during the first half of the 2nd century B.C. But this flourishing artistic activity soon came to an end, for the aristocracy stopped commissioning works, so anxious were they to become an integral part of the Roman state. Evidence of this can be found in the portraits of local magistrates, commissioned by themselves, on urns dating from the early 1st century and also in the history of the *Ceicna*-Caecina family.

POPULONIA is the only Etruscan city that even the ancient geographers considered anomalous for its position on the sea. It owed its prosperity, which lasted uninterruptedly from the archaic period to late Hellenism, to the mineral resources in the area of Campiglia and on the island of Elba: the maritime transportation of these minerals made its port the most developed of the area. On the coast of the bay of Baratti, Villanovan necropolises, belonging to two separate communities, have been found at Poggio del Molino, Poggio alla Porcareccia, San Cerbone and at Granate. These show close links

93

94

95

with the culture of the Nuraghe, perhaps brought here by Phoenician traders. As early as the end of the 9th century B.C. they were building chamber tombs for multiple burials, covered by a dome made by progressively projecting stone slabs. Between the mid-8th and the mid-7th centuries, contact with Greek merchants in search of mineral ore does not seem to have brought much prosperity to the region, probably because this trade was mediated by the more powerful (and more socially evolved) communities of southern Etruria. Despite this, in the first half of the 7th century some large mound tombs were built (for example, those of the Flabelli or of the Carri, which can be seen in that part of the necropolis that is open to the public). The marvellous collection of objects found here is evidence of a rigidly aristocratic and warrior ideology: iron weapons, andirons, grills and locally manufactured chariots. From the last decades of the 7th century and throughout the 6th, the number of imported artifacts (Etruscan-Corinthian, Corinthian, Greek-Oriental and Attic ceramics) which have been found in the tombs—from the earliest mound tombs, to the *aediculae*, to the sarcophagi, to the *cassone* tombs—increased considerably; it also reflects an acquaintance with Greek-Oriental culture which influences even the local artistic activities, such as the acroteria and the palm-shaped decorations at the top of stone steles (examples in the Archaeological Museum in Florence and in the local museum).

Towards the middle of the 6th century the necropolises were all transferred to the flat stretch of coast along the bay and a set of walls was built (in part still standing), which enclosed the two *poggi* (hills), Poggio del Molino and Poggio del Castello. This leads us to

92. Volterra, the arched gate (3rd-2nd century B.C.).

93. Alabaster urn from Volterra (late 3rd century B.C.). Vatican, Gregorian Etruscan Museum. On the lid, the deceased couple; on the base, Pelops kills Enomaos. The style shows the influence of the art of Pergamon.

94. Bronze coin from the Volterra mint, reverse side (3rd century B.C.). Along the rim, the inscription Velathri (Volterra); at the centre, a dolphin and the symbol of its value. Volterra, Guarnacci Museum.

95. Bronze statuette of a warrior (from Populonia, first half of the 5th century B.C.). Florence, Archaeological Museum.

Metallurgy

The science of metallurgy reached Italy during the 3rd millennium B.C. and is documented at first by copper and arsenic daggers and flat axes, as well as by traces of mining activities found in Tuscany and Trentino. During the Bronze Age, the use of metal was widespread, not only for weapons but also for tools (axes, sickles) and ornaments (collars, brooches, bracelets). The many stone moulds that have been found prove that the processing also took place locally.

Traces of mining activity have been found in the area around Massa Marittima and Campiglia, where the smelting furnaces for iron and copper were placed near the mines (the ones at Val Fucinaia, at Campiglia, in use from the 8th century B.C. onwards, are open to the public). The iron ore mined on the island of Elba, on the other hand, was processed at Populonia after the 6th century.

In the 8th and 7th centuries B.C. metal objects were manufactured almost exclusively at Vetulonia, Vulci, Tarquinia and Caere; the old procedure of thinly hammered layers, joined together with rivets, was used. Later, after the 6th-5th century, the workshops in southern Etruria (Vulci, Caere, Volsinii) and those in inland northern Etruria learnt from the Greeks the practice of soldering and began to make more use of the casting procedure, specially in the production of vases. These innovations led, on the one hand, to much shorter production times and increased quantities, making Etruscan produce competitive on other Italian and central European markets; and on the other made it possible to create large-scale statues, of which the Mars from Todi, the Chimaera and the Orator are the only surviving examples.

We have very little information about mining activity in Roman times, and what little we have has yet to be properly studied. The processing of iron, the most common metal in Etruria, probably continued much as before. At Populonia, an analysis of the quantity of iron present in the scrap—much more than in the previous period—would seem to indicate a much faster but less accurate processing technique. According to the information we have today, iron processing in Populonia increased in the 3rd and 2nd centuries,

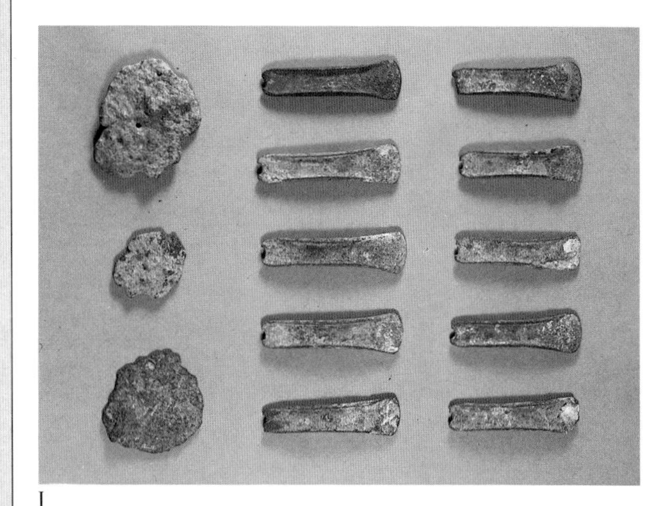
I

II

III

IV

probably because of the increase in demand from Rome. Pliny mentions Populonia's vast contribution of iron to Rome at the time of the second Punic war. But in the 1st century iron processing seems to fall off quite suddenly, more or less at the same time as the development of metallurgical activities in Carnia, in the Alps. The copper mines of Vetulonia and Populonia, and the cinnabar (used for leagues) ones on Mount Amiata, appear to have suffered the same fate, probably because of the competition afforded by the mines in the Iberian peninsula.

V

I. Bronze axes and ingots (from Campiglia Marittima, early Bronze Age). Florence, Archaeological Museum.

II. Bronze lamina cart (from the Olmo Bello necropolis, Bisenzio, second half of the 8th century B.C.). Rome, Villa Giulia.

III. Bronze lamina throne with relief decoration (from the Barberini tomb at Preneste, first half of the 7th century B.C.). Rome, Villa Giulia.

IV. Relief showing a blacksmith's workshop. Aquileia, Archaeological Museum.

V. Bronze statue of a Chimaera, with a votive inscription (from Arezzo, early 4th century B.C.). Florence, Archaeological Museum.

96

98

97

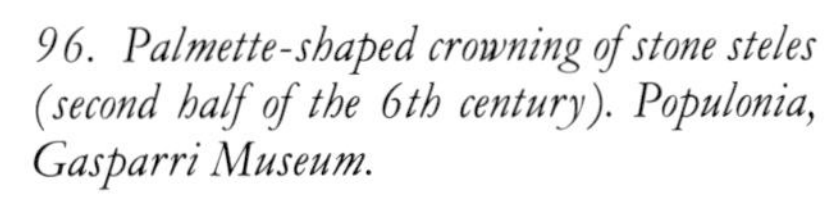

96. Palmette-shaped crowning of stone steles (second half of the 6th century). Populonia, Gasparri Museum.

97. Populonia, Archaic walls (around the mid-6th century B.C.).

98. Populonia, aedicula and cassone tombs (6th-5th century B.C.). In the foreground, the aedicula tomb known as the 'tomb of the bronze statuette making an offering.'

99. Populonia, Porcareccia necropolis, Flabelli tumulus, with two stone steles in front of the entrance (second half of the 7th century B.C.).

99

believe that the community had become a city and it is significant that it should have happened at the same time as the processing of the minerals from Elba became publicly administered. An industrial factory was built for this purpose outside the city, at Poggio alla Porcareccia; it contained also housing for the workers and was used until the beginning of the 3rd century B.C. Also at this time Populonia began to coin its own money, an indispensable instrument for the development of the metal trade; it coined sporadically at first, but began to issue regular series (coins with Gorgon head) at the beginning of the 4th century and continued through to the middle of the 3rd.

The city's prosperity continued during the 5th and 4th centuries, as is shown by the importation of ceramics from Attica (the two hydrias by the painter Meidias in the Archaeological Museum in Florence are remarkable), and later from Latium, southern Etruria and

Campania. Not even the two expeditions led by the Syracusans in 453 B.C. against the mining district seem to have caused much damage.

It was during the 4th century that the industry of metal processing reached its peak, as can be deduced from the vast accumulation of scrap that buried the old necropolis. At the same time, the city became very powerful politically, as is shown by the construction of a new set of walls with towers (visible along the road leading to the castle) that isolated the whole promontory from the mainland. Also at this time, the new hilltop fortresses on the island of Elba were built to protect the mines. During the 3rd century, Populonia must have joined the system of alliances with Rome and in 205 B.C. the city supplied iron for Scipio's campaign in Africa. During the 2nd century, the port continued its activity of metal trade, but the processing had by then been transferred to Puteoli (Pozzuoli).

100

101

102

100. Volterra, the Roman theatre (1st century A.D.).

101. Volterra, the steps of the Roman theatre.

102. Volterra, the mosaic floor of the baths (1st century A.D.).

During the civil war VOLTERRA sided with Marius and this caused Sulla's revenge: in 80-79 B.C. he besieged the city and eventually conquered it, depriving the inhabitants of Roman citizenship. But it does not seem that Sulla then transformed the city into a colony, as happened in many other parts of Etruria.

The construction of the major public buildings is due to the most important local families. The theatre, for example, was built in the early 1st century A.D. by A. Caecina Severus and his son Sixtus. At the foot of the stage there were statues of Roman emperors (at the Guarnacci Museum there are two statues of Augustus and one of Livia). The names inscribed on the seats—among which the name of the family of the poet Persius—provide interesting material for the study of the local notables. The theatre was modernized and restored several times during the 1st and 2nd centuries, and in the 3rd century it was definitively abandoned and used as a rubbish dump. Behind the stage there is a large portico and a building housing baths. A large cistern which supplied water to the whole city dates from the Augustan period. Just outside Porta San Felice, on the Acropolis, there are the ruins of baths and private houses (some floor mosaics can be seen in the Guarnacci Museum).

We know very little about the territory around Volterra, for it has not yet been studied systematically. Research has recently been undertaken at the villas of San Vincenzino and San Gaetano at Vada. But we can state fairly certainly that there were many large landed estates based on slave labour, as was common in northern Etruria, while the areas further south were divided into smaller properties.

We have very little information about POPULONIA in Roman times. We know that the city supplied iron for Scipio's campaign in Africa (205 B.C.). Coins dating from the 2nd century B.C. prove that at the time the city was still in existence. But the imperial age must have brought a rapid decline, and we know that Strabo saw the city in a state of total abandon, inhabited only by workers involved in the metal industries. The production of iron, which had been particularly intensive during the middle and late republican period (and perhaps even slightly later), has left us seven metres of accumulated

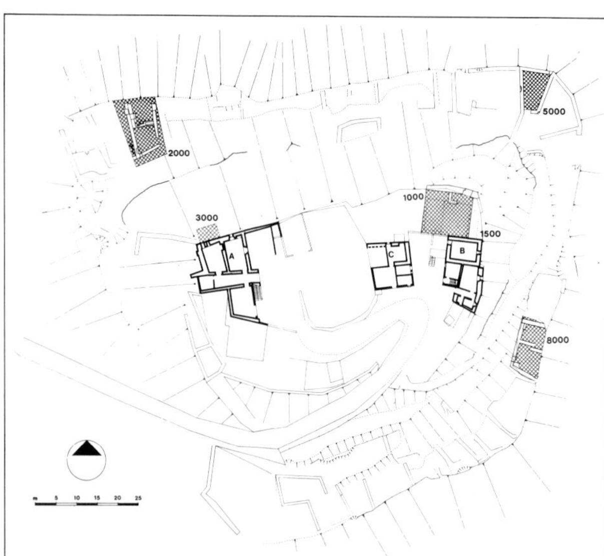

103. Montarrenti, 12th-century tower belonging to the castle keep (B on the plan). To the left, the excavations (1000 on the plan) reveal the late medieval constructions.

104. Montarrenti, the peasants' village (5000 on the plan). Under the late medieval constructions we can see the holes for the beams of the early medieval houses.

105. Ground-plan of the castle of Montarrenti. At the centre, the buildings forming the castle keep, surrounded by the peasants' village.

106. Melted bronze belt cap and disc-shaped gold fibula (from Volterra, late 7th century). Florence, Archaeological Museum.

scrap along the coast of the bay of Baratti. There are ruins of a few seaside villas along the coast of the promontory. Among these, worthy of mention is the one of Poggio del Molino, where scholars of the last century found a Nilotic mosaic dating from the first half of the 1st century B.C. (sold, outside Italy, to private antique dealers). In the museum of Populonia there are some inscriptions dating from the Roman period.

The town of SIENA (*Saena*), which probably became a colony under Augustus, grew up on the site of a previous settlement, possibly an Etruscan community called *Saina*. The town never really became important, despite its favourable position along the Cassian Way. Very few materials have been found; they are in the local archaeological museum and among them is a portrait of the so-called Pseudo-Seneca. The recent discovery of some Roman period pottery suggests, among other things, that the centre of the town was near Castelvecchio. Lower down, more or less where today's Piazza del Campo stands, there was the city's forum—which was called *campus fori*. There are ruins of villas on the surrounding territory (at Vico Bello, Pieve al Bozzone and La Befa), but they all seem to have been quite small. They must, however, have survived until quite late, probably from the Augustan period until the 5th century A.D.

The bishopric of SIENA was from the very beginning one of the smallest in Tuscany, surrounded as it was by the two great dioceses of Volterra and Arezzo. The latter practically reached as far as the gates of the city itself. This was the result of the different degree of importance of these cities in the Roman period. During the first years of the Longobard occupation, Siena had no bishop, but its military and administrative territory grew considerably, at the expense of Arezzo. This fact underlies the numerous territorial quarrels between the two dioceses which were only definitively resolved in the early 13th century when it was decided that the churches of the area, claimed by Siena, were to be considered under the administration of Arezzo. Some of these churches still house interesting fragments of early medieval sculpture. The economic development of Siena was due to its position along the *Via Francigena.*

Very few materials dating from the early Middle Ages, mostly housed in the Archaeological Museum in Siena, have been found in the area of the city; traces of "pre-Romanesque" settlements in the countryside are equally few and far between. Only recently the excavation of the castle of MONTARRENTI (dicoese of Volterra) has provided us with some archaeological information. It is a typical example of a fortified village, the centre of the administration of a landed estate, and its existence is documented from the mid-12th century. Today Montarrenti consists of the vast ruins of a castle keep, with two towers and other houses, and an abandoned town below, enclosed by a set of walls. The houses, inhabited until the late Middle Ages by peasants and sharecroppers, show that the land had been regularly divided up. The excavation of the upper part and a partial study of the town have shown that the settlement, during its earliest stages (9th-10th centuries), consisted of irregular buildings, partly in wood, spread over the whole area of the later castle, without any "town-planning" as such.

VETULONIA AND RUSELLAE

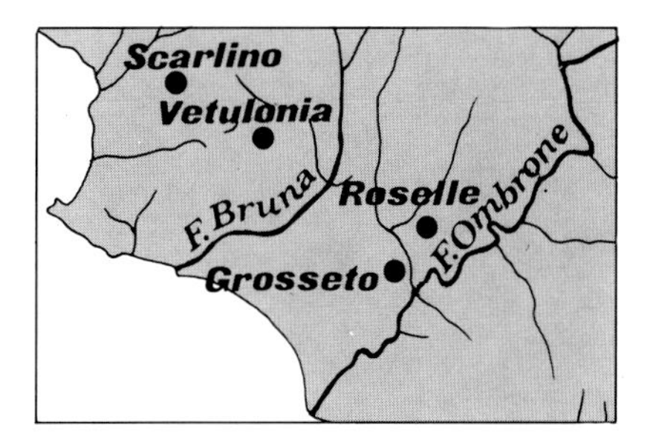

The lower Palaeolithic is represented by bifacial implements found at Pian dell'Osa; the Middle and Upper Palaeolithic, by surface finds throughout the territory, in the Grotta La Fabbrica at Alberese, in the Grotta Cala Giovanna at Pianosa (Civic Museum of Reggio Emilia), and by surface finds on the island of Elba. In the Grotta Vado all'Arancio near Massa Marittima there were Gravettian tombs, with several interesting artifacts, including a human profile (Florentine Prehistorical Museum). From the Neolithic period a few impressed ceramics have been found at Elba and Pianosa, while the documentation of the Aeneolithic and the Bronze Age is much greater: traces of mining activities in the cinnabar lodes on Mount Amiata, burials in artificial small grottoes at Pianosa and in natural grottoes elsewhere, such as Grotta San Giuseppe at Rio Marina on Elba (Antiquarium of Marciana Marina), Grotta dello Scoglietto (Florentine Prehistorical Museum), small grottoes at Pianizzoli and Prato (Civic Museum at Massa Marittima), Grotta del Fontino (objects at the Florentine Prehistorical Museum). The later periods are documented by ruins dating from the Appennine culture on Mount Amiata and by the proto-Villanovan necropolis at Sticciano Scalo (Civic Museum at Grosseto and Archaeological Museum in Florence).

VETULONIA prospered thanks to the mineral resources afforded by the Colline Metallifere and its fortunate position on the lagoon of Lake Prile (now drained). The Villanovan necropolises on the surrounding hills belonged to two distinct communities; the objects from the earliest period found in them are very modest. But from

107

10

108

107. Funerary vase (from Grotta San Giuseppe, Island of Elba, Aeneolithic). Pisa, Institute of Anthropology.

108. Bell-shaped vases and bone buttons (from Grotta del Fontino, Aeneolithic). Florence, Florentine Prehistorical Museum.

109. Vetulonia, Tomba del Diavolino, a tumulus tomb with a square chamber topped by a false vault supported by a central pilaster (around 620-600 B.C.).

the middle of the 8th century onwards there was an increase in the wealth of the inhabitants: ambers were imported from the north, Nuraghic materials from Sardinia and glass paste and a Phoenician cup from the Orient (Archaeological Museum in Florence; some examples in the local Antiquarium). The necropolis, and by this stage also the settlement by the Lake of Accesa (Civic Museum of Massa Marittima), show that the community of Vetulonia began very early on to administer the metal trade, perhaps through the mediation of Vulci or Tarquinia. Soon metal processing was also done locally. The "Oriental" style tombs (7th century), consisting of several ditches within a single circle of stones, were filled with real treasures: gold jewellery and precious vases imported from southern Etruria and the Orient, Greek ceramics, Oriental bronze cauldrons and elegant products of the local metal industry (tripods, cauldrons, bronze incense burners, gold objects; Archaeological Museum in Florence). Dating from the second half of the 7th century there are huge chamber tombs, topped by false vaults sustained by pilasters. Among these the tombs of Diavolino and Pietrera are open to the public.

Towards the middle of the 6th century B.C., when the city walls were built, Vetulonia began to show signs of decline, as can be deduced from the necropolis; perhaps its role as mining centre was being taken over by the growing town of Populonia. On the other hand, prosperity appears to have continued uninterruptedly both in the aristocratic countryside tumulus tomb at Poggio Pelliccia near Gavorrano (with burials from the mid-7th to the early 5th century B.C.) and in a building in the city, possibly a temple, at Costa Murata, where Etruscan and Greek ceramics from the early 6th to the mid-5th centuries have been found.

The city of RUSELLAE (Roselle) began to be important around the middle of the 6th century. Since we have found no interesting artifacts of local production, Rusellae's power must have been based on the control over the valley of the Ombrone and on agricultural

111

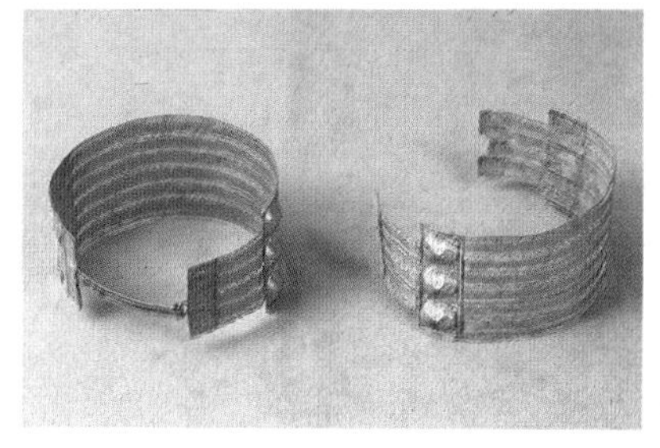

112

113

110. Head of a stone statue of a woman (from the tumulus of Pietrera at Vetulonia, 650-625 B.C.) Florence, Archaeological Museum. The style of the sculpture clearly shows the influence of small-scale Oriental sculpture.

111. Vetulonia, tumulus of Pietrera (650-625 B.C.).

112. Two gold bracelets (from the tumulus of Migliarine at Vetulonia, 620-600 B.C.). Florence, Archaeological Museum. These were made in a local workshop, using the filigree technique.

113. Two bronze horse's bits, produced locally (from the necropolis of Lake Accesa, second half of the 8th century B.C.). Massa Marittima, Archaeological Museum.

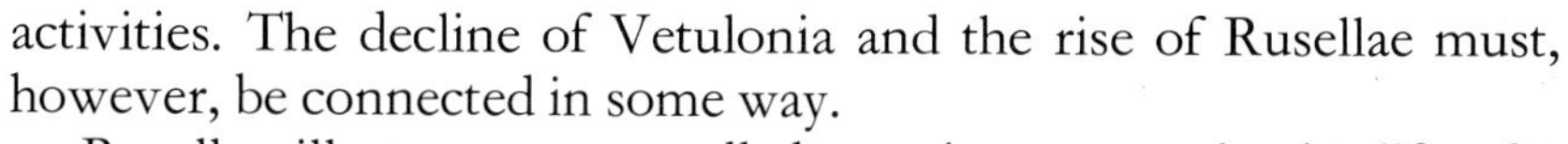

activities. The decline of Vetulonia and the rise of Rusellae must, however, be connected in some way.

Rusellae illustrates very well the various stages in the life of a town of ancient Etruria: from the 7th century B.C. (the date of the oldest house) to the 9th century A.D., when the Christian basilica was built. We know very little about the necropolises, for no systematic excavations have yet been made; but we can get an idea of the grandeur of the city by the enormous set of cyclopean stone walls (mid-6th century B.C.), marking the birth of the city as such, also documented by the presence of contemporary architectural terracottas, similar to the ones found at Murlo, in the upper valley of the Ombrone. The prosperity of Rusellae is shown in the 5th century by the importation of Attic ceramics, and in the Hellenistic period by the restoration of the walls, the new houses built on the southern hillside and by the construction of a temple in the 2nd century, documented by architectural terracottas in the Microasiatic style.

According to Silius Italicus, it was VETULONIA that handed down to Rome the usage of emblems of power, such as the *fasci* or the curule chair; but Vetulonia, during the Roman period, was no more than an insignificant *municipium*.

Ceramics Workshops

During the Neolithic period and the metal ages pottery was made by hand and cooked over an open fire; the lathe was not used until the late Bronze Age. Several kinds of ceramics were produced: from rough clay ones with only vaguely smoothed surfaces, to fine red or black polished ones, yellow vessels made of the finest clay, generally painted red or brown.

The Etruscans' production of ceramics, between the 9th and 2nd centuries, developed continuously in terms of quantity; it could be manufactured in the home by the women, or on a large scale in organized workshops. From the technological point of view, a qualitative development occurred around the middle of the 8th century when contact with the first Greek colonizers introduced the use of the lathe and the practice of refining clay. From this time onward, ceramics were produced by specialized workers who often signed their works. Until the 3rd century, Etruscan ceramics were imitations of Greek models, and took on their shapes, names and decorations: Etruscan geometric ceramics (8th century), Etruscan-Corinthian (7th-6th), Ionic style (6th), Attic and Magna Graecian red-figure vases (5th-4th), Attic and Campanian black varnish (4th-3rd). Even bucchero, a typically Etruscan black ceramic based on local traditions, was influenced by imported models in its shapes and decorations (Phoenician, Corinthian, Greek Oriental styles).

I

II

III

Among the various different types of ceramics produced in Etruria, some were intended primarily for export (black varnish ceramics and fine drinking cups) and others were used locally or regionally (common use ceramics and *dolia*). Pratically none of the workshops that produced these vases have been identified, except the ones in Arezzo which were located inside the city walls. Thanks to the numerous and varied trade marks stamped on the vases, we are able to reconstruct the organization of these factories. In Arezzo, where about ninety different workshops have been identified, the workers were slaves and their numbers varied according to the size of the factory. In some cases there was only one slave, in others ten or twenty, and in some even sixty. In the larger workshops the internal division of labour must have relied on a complex organization, requiring some slaves to fulfil rather generic functions, while others were truly specialized workers. The processing, in fact, went from the simplest tasks, such as the digging of clay or the storage of the vases, to the more complicated procedures of refining the clay and varnishing and baking the pots; the most difficult and delicate tasks were naturally the modelling and the decoration of the vases. These jobs were done by highly specialized slaves who signed each vase with their personal stamp, and it is these markings that have made this reconstruction possible. The procedure, however, was not always like this. The trademarks on vases produced elsewhere, even though in imitation of the ones made at Arezzo ("Italic" or "late Italic" ceramics), are not the signatures of the individual craftsman, but more generally of the manufacturing "company." It is likely that this indicates a different labour organization, but we still know too little about it to be certain. The systematic excavation of some of the workshops found in Arezzo would help to answer this question and many others as well.

After the 6th century A.D. ceramic production declined enormously; the lavish late Roman sets of tableware disappeared and the only kinds of pottery used were a few kitchen objects, such as the jar and the dish (which was

IV

V

essential for the cooking of farinaceous foods and began to be used at this time), and the table tankard. None of them were glazed and their decoration, if any, consisted in simple wavey line patterns. The Longobards used mainly pottery produced locally, even as burial objects; this explains why in Etruria no pots like the ones from the northern Italian necropolises have been found, and only a few objects imported from North Africa or from central Europe (Museum of Fiesole). This situation remained constant until at least the 12th century.

This decline in ceramic production denotes a change in the manufacturing organization: the large, almost industrially organized production centres must have disappeared, while small workshops, covering a small market, spread and in some cases the production was even handled "in the home." It was not until the birth of late medieval enamel factories in Orvieto, Viterbo, Pisa, Montelupo and Siena that production increased enough for Tuscany to become a centre of ceramics export again.

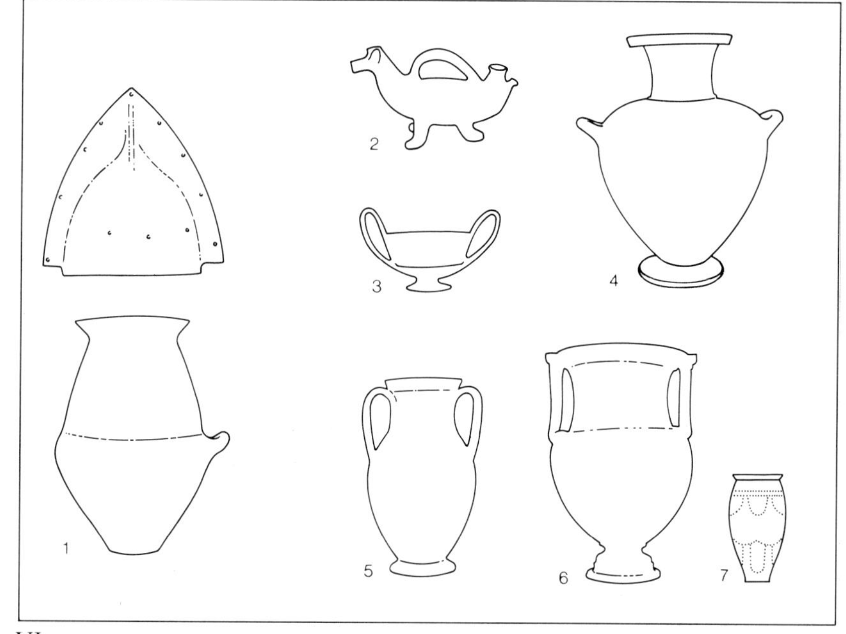

VI

VII

VIII

IX

X

I. Appennine culture ceramics (from Grotta dell'Orso, Sarteano, Bronze Age). Florence, Archaeological Museum.

II. Proto-Villanovan ossuary (from Sticciano Scalo) and bowl (from Grotta dell'Orso, Sarteano, Bronze Age). Florence, Archaeological Museum.

III. Etruscan-Corinthian amphora, decorated with friezes of animals by the so-called Painter of the Bearded Sphynx (from Vulci, late 7th century B.C.). Rome, Villa Giulia.

IV. Bucchero bucket with relief decorations showing a frieze of animals, influenced by Syrian and Phoenician models (from Caere, 650-625 B.C.). Rome, Villa Giulia.

V. Crater by the so-called Painter of Dawn (from Falerii, 375-350 B.C.). Rome, Villa Giulia. On this side, Dawn rising out of the sea on a chariot drawn by four horses; seated next to her is her lover Titon.

VI. Reconstruction of Etruscan ceramics. This drawing illustrates the different kinds of Etruscan ceramics from the 9th to the 2nd centuries B.C.

1. *9th century B.C.*
2. *8th century B.C.*
3. *7th century B.C.*
4. *6th century B.C.*
5. *5th century B.C.*
6. *4th-3rd centuries B.C.*
7. *2nd century B.C.*

VII. A mould for "Aretini" vases (1st century B.C.). Arezzo, Archaeological Museum.

VIII. An "Aretino" vase (1st century B.C.–1st century A.D.). Arezzo, Archaeological Museum.

IX. Unpainted ceramic tankards (from Fiesole, 10th-11th century). Fiesole, Archaeological Museum.

X. Ceramic bottles (from Fiesole, 7th century). Fiesole, Archaeological Museum. These objects are very similar to the ones that were produced in the lower valley of the Rhein at the same time.

1

116

118

114. Rusellae, the city walls (mid-6th century B.C., with later additions).

115. Rusellae, aerial view of the excavations.

116. Statue of a young girl (Rusellae, 1st century A.D.). Grosseto, Archaeological Museum.

117. Rusellae, view of the excavations.

118. Gold earring (first half of the 7th century). Grosseto, Archaeological Museum.

RUSELLAE, on the other hand, was a very important centre of this region and we have far more information about it. The earliest records tell us of the war with Rome in the early 3rd century B.C., which lasted a few years and ended with Rome's conquest of the city. We also know that Rusellae supplied wheat to Scipio's campaign in Africa (205 B.C.). The town became a *municipium* and, later, under Augustus, a colony. It seems that at this time the city was reduced to a much smaller area, concentrated around the forum. Thanks to the ruins brought to light by the excavations begun in the 1950's, we have discovered that in the Augustan period a space was flattened in order to create a plateau where the forum was built. The forum consisted of a square in the centre, with no paving. The square was crossed by a little cobblestone road; another similar road ran along the west side of the square. On this side, large terracing walls supported a portico. The whole area was eventually flattened out in the 1st century A.D. and from this time on several changes took place: the existing buildings were restored and enlarged and many new ones were built. A paved road was constructed along the east side of the square, possibly following the course of the *cardo maximus* (the main street running along the north-south axis). At the north-east corner of the square, this street turned east at right angles, thus becoming a *decumanus* (east-west axis). This is quite unusual, for normally there were two or more streets that intersected perpendicularly. At the corner, where the street curved sharply, there was probably a fountain. The basilica, on the east side of the square, was rectangular in plan; it had a raised entrance atrium with steps leading up to it. The internal space was surrounded by rows of columns, eight on the long sides and four on the short ones. The original construction of the basilica would appear to date from the Augustan period, whereas the raised entrance hall, with its very different building techniques, cannot have been built before the imperial age. The seat of the *Augustales* (a body of six men who organized the worship of Augustus and were elected annually) stood along the short side of the square. This building was rectangular, and its walls were covered with marble slabs; near the apse, two stone bases have been found, which probably supported the statues of Augustus and Livia. In the niches along the long sides there were probably statues of members of the Julian-Claudian dynasty (several of these are in the Archaeological Museum in Grosseto). Rusellae's decline began in the 2nd century.

Despite the economic and social transformations that characterized the territory of the Maremma from the late imperial age onward, and despite the decline of the city itself, RUSELLAE was the seat of the diocese from the 5th century until it was transferred to Grosseto in 1138. The Longobard necropolises scattered over the territory indicate that the city had a very small population; this is also confirmed by the fact that only one important public building was constructed over the whole period: the Christian basilica. Built on Roman ruins, it consists of a nave and two aisles, with a raised narthex and presbytery and a square apse with two rooms leading off it. Reliefs and pilasters, decorated with guilloches, swastikas and rosettes (8th-9th centuries), covered the lefthand wall of the apse.

But the most interesting objects come from the Longobard necropolis of Casette di Mota (a few hundred yards south of Rusellae), consisting of fourteen tombs, and from the larger necropolis of Grangia, probably connected to the town of Montecavoli (on a hill a few miles south of Grosseto). The study of this necropolis has revealed that only the central and earliest nucleus of tombs contained personal objects. The personal objects belonging to women in the tombs of Grangia consist mainly in disc-shaped fibulas, one of which has an ornament in the centre, cross-shaped fibulas and pearls; the men's objects are mostly bronze ornaments for belts, buckles and shield decorations. All these objects can be dated at the 7th century in analogy with similar materials found north of the Alps.

VULCI, SOVANA AND COSA

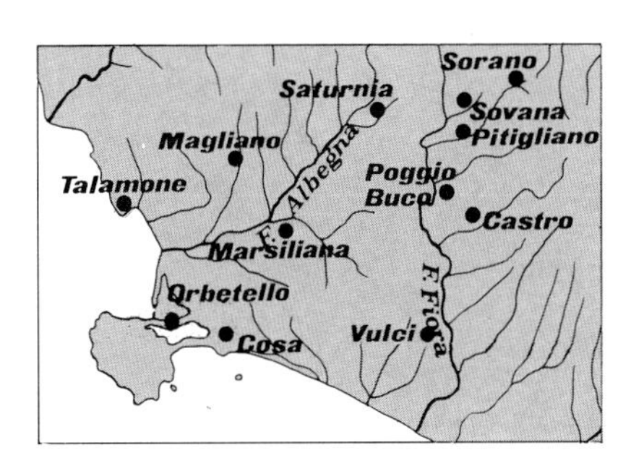

From the Palaeolithic period there are shards found at Montauto di Manciano; from the Mousterian culture, at Cala dei Santi and Settefinestre. Apart from the Neolithic fragments found at Vulci, it is not until the Aeneolithic period that we find any evidence of communities represented by tombs in artificial small grottoes (Rinaldone culture) found especially in the valley of the Fiora (the "Tomb of the Widow" has been reconstructed at the Pigorini Museum in Rome) between Pitigliano, Manciano, Capalbio and Garavicchio, and at Farnese. The bell-shaped vases found at Torre Crognola (Vulci) and the burial

119

12

119. Funerary objects (from Ponte San Pietro, Viterbo, Eneolithic). Florence, Archaeological Museum.

120. Vulci, Ponte della Badia, on the river Fiora (first half of the 1st century B.C.).

grottoes at Punta degli Stretti (Argentario) and at Sassi Neri (Capalbio) appear to indicate the transition to the Bronze Age, characterized in its earliest stage by stores of bronze objects (Manciano, Montemerano and Saturnia) and by the pile-dwellings on Lake Mezzano. The later periods are represented by villages along the Fiora (Ponte San Pietro, Crostoletto di Lamone) and by evidence of worship of water and agricultural deities in grottoes. The number of settlements increased greatly in the proto-Villanovan age: many villages sprang up, often on the site of existing ones, and they were characterized by stone walls and huts and by tumulus tombs. Among the most interesting are Crostoletto di Lamone, Sorgenti della Nova and Bisenzio. Objects are at the Villa Giulia Museum and Pigorini Museum in Rome, at the museum in Vulci and at the Antiquarium in Saturnia.

The vast territory that eventually fell under the rule of VULCI—the valleys of the Fiora and of the Albegna—is indicative of the relationship between city and countryside in southern Etruria. During the early Villanovan period (9th century B.C.) and for most of the later (8th century), our information comes almost entirely from the area of the future city, with the four necropolises of Osteria, Cavalupo, Cuccumella and Polledrara, which continued to be used even in the following centuries (materials in the Antiquarium of Castello della Badia and in the Villa Giulia Museum in Rome; particularly interesting is a small bronze statue of Nuraghic origin found at Cavalupo, proving that trade with Sardinia began very early). During the second half of the 8th century the aristocracy of Vulci must have been in close contact with the Greek colonizers, probably because they controlled the routes towards the mines of northern Etruria. This contact is shown by the presence in Vulci of Euboean ceramics, brought here by the Greek colonizers of Pitecusa (Ischia), such as the krater from Pescia Romana (Grosseto Museum), and by the

121

122

123

121. Euboean crater, decorated with geometric patterns (from Pescia Romana, around 720 B.C.). Grosseto, Archaeological Museum.

122. Tyrrhenian amphora (from Vulci, 575-550 B.C.). Vatican, Gregorian Etruscan Museum. This type of ceramic vase, produced by Athenian craftsmen exclusively for the Etruscan market, was considered a luxury item. In the top frieze, Hercules struggles with the centaur; in the others, animal scenes.

123. Saturnia, Puntone necropolis, Tomb A, a tumulus with a square chamber and slab walls (675-650 B.C.).

imitations produced locally by immigrant craftsmen (such as the biconical ossuary in the Antiquarium in Vulci).

During this period the investment of excess wealth led to the first agrarian appropriations and numerous aristocratic citadels sprang up throughout the territory (Castro, Poggio Buco, Pitigliano, Sovana, Saturnia, Marsiliana, Magliano, Orbetello), all of them placed in strategic positions controlling the communication routes. There are many necropolises in these areas, some of which are open to the public. One of these is the one at POGGIO BUCO, with ditch graves and chamber tombs, some of which consisting of several rooms, with sculpted pilasters and support beams, showing the influence of Caere. In the necropolis of CASTRO, the chamber tombs are decorated with stone sculptures in the shape of real and imaginary animals; a unique entrance path to one of the tombs is lined on both sides by rows of animal statues; a large altar is topped by tufa cornices decorated in the corners with heads of rams and lions (materials in the Antiquarium of Ischia di Castro). At SATURNIA one can visit the necropolis of Pian di Palma, with tumulus tombs built out of stone slabs. But the most prosperous of all those communities appears to have been MARSILIANA, in a strategic position for the control of the routes to the Colline Metallifere; in its tombs at Banditella, (ditch graves within stone circles), were the burial sites of warriors accompanied by remarkable personal objects, especially the "Circolo della Fibula" and the "Circolo degli Avori" in the Archaeological Museum in Florence. These objects are more interesting even than those found in contemporary tombs at Vulci, such as the Tomb of the Chariot (Tomba del Carro) with its embossed bronze foils, now in the Villa Giulia Museum in Rome.

The destruction of Marsiliana in the late 7th century, and the gradual decline over the course of the next century of the other towns, mark the definitive supremacy of the city over the countryside. This historical event is recalled also in the paintings of the François tomb, where among the enemies of the heroes of Vulci,

124

125

127

126

124. Vulci, late republican period house.

125. Vulci, Roman street.

126. Vulci, late republican period house.

127. Statue of a centaur in tufa stone (from the necropolis of Poggio Maremma; Vulci, early 6th century B.C.). Rome, Villa Giulia. In Vulci, statues of real and imaginary animals were placed as guardians in front of the entrance to the tombs.

Avile and *Caile Vipinas*, there is also a warrior from Sovana. Vulci's period of greatest prosperity lasted from the late 7th century to the mid-5th, as is shown by the numerous chamber tombs (exceptional is the one at Cuccumella, a tumulus, with an inner chamber with steps) containing Greek-Oriental and Corinthian ceramics, and later Attic and Ionic ones (materials in the Antiquarium in Vulci and in the Villa Giulia Museum, in particular the tomb of Panatenaica). During this period many workshops producing ceramics were set up, often by Greek craftsmen such as the Painter of Swallows, a Greek-Oriental (bowl in the Villa Giulia Museum), or the Painter of the Bearded Sphinx, of Corinthian origin (objects from the tomb of the same name at Villa Giulia), or later, after the mid-6th century, by craftsmen of Ionic origin. Also remarkable during the 6th and 5th centuries is the sculpture (see such masterpieces as the centaur and the sea-horse at Villa Giulia) and the production of bronze vases and implements (for example, the Warrior's Tomb, late 6th century, at Villa Giulia). Objects produced at Vulci were exported to distant lands, as is shown by the precious objects, such as decorated ostrich eggs, found in northern Etruria and in the Marches, by the ceramics of the "Ciclo dei Rosoni" found in Carthage and Provence, by the bronzes found all over Etruria proper, in Campanian and Po Valley Etruria, in non-Greek areas of southern Italy and in central-northern Europe, and above all by the wine amphoras found all over the western Mediterranean, indicating also that Vulci had a flourishing and specialized agricultural activity.

After the decline of coastal southern Etruria in the second half of the 5th century, Vulci took part in the renaissance of the 4th cen-

28

129

130

tury. New public works were built, such as the walls and the great temple (ruins open to the public); new aristocratic tombs, with T-shaped central chambers (at Ponte Rotto), and magnificent burial sites dug out of the rock, with *aedicula* facades (sculpted tympanums in the Antiquarium). The François tomb, dating from the second half of the 4th century, is particularly interesting. The paintings that decorated it (transferred to Villa Albani in Rome in 1857, shortly after their discovery) show the influence of Apulian painting. They illustrate a complex story, in which the killing of the Trojan prisoners by Achilles and other characters from Greek mythology is interspersed with duels beween the heroes of Vulci and warriors from Rome, Sovana, Volsinii and Falerii. These battles, although in the fiction of the paintings taking place in the distant past (late 6th century), must have been intended as symbolic of the struggle of southern Etruscan cities against Rome. The two most famous sculpted sarcophagi, with a couple lying on the lid, are in Boston; another, illustrating a battle between Amazons, is now at the Villa Giulia Museum.

During this period, as happened elsewhere in southern Etruria, the towns that had prospered during the archaic age experienced a new development. Among these, SOVANA, where new elaborate tombs were constructed in the rock of the hillside; many of them are now open to the public, such as the Tomb of Hildebrand (first half of the 3rd century), carved into the rock in the shape of a temple, with beautifully ornamented capitals, or the Tomb of the Siren and the picturesque pathway, called Cavone, with Etruscan inscriptions on the walls. Sovana and the other smaller towns continued to thrive even after Vulci began to decline. Vulci was defeated by Q. Coruncanius in 280 B.C. and a large part of its territory was confiscated. But the smaller towns were favoured by Roman policy which

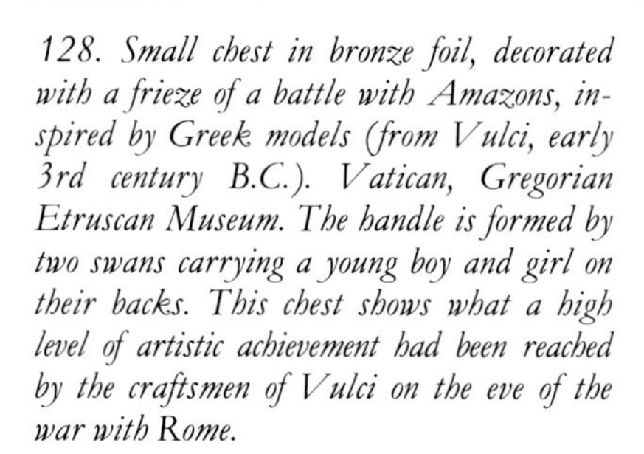

128. Small chest in bronze foil, decorated with a frieze of a battle with Amazons, inspired by Greek models (from Vulci, early 3rd century B.C.). Vatican, Gregorian Etruscan Museum. The handle is formed by two swans carrying a young boy and girl on their backs. This chest shows what a high level of artistic achievement had been reached by the craftsmen of Vulci on the eve of the war with Rome.

129. Pediment of the temple of Talamone, detail showing Oedipus. Florence, Archaeological Museum. The temple was rebuilt and modernized in the first half of the 2nd century B.C. in accordance with the Roman policy of strengthening the outposts of the territory around Vulci.

130. Sovana, Hildebrand Tomb, facade in the style of a temple (first half of the 3rd century B.C.).

Trade

The existence of trade is documented during the Palaeolithic period by the use of flint from distant countries and by the presence of non-indigenous sea-shells. During the Neolithic, obsidian was imported from Lipari, Sardinia and the Aegean islands. During the Bronze Age, Italy was involved in the exchanges between northern Europe and Mycenae and took part in the trade of metals and amber.

From the middle of the 8th century to the end of 7th, Etruria exchanged with foreign merchants, who were often integrated in Etruscan society, mineral products for luxury items (ceramics, jewellery, precious metal vases), precious raw materials (gold, silver, ivory, amber) and agricultural produce (oil and wine). After the late 7th century, the Etruscans began to play an active role in maritime trade, exporting wine and pottery (jugs and goblets) to the western Mediterranean countries. Their presence in the eastern Mediterranean is documented by the spread of "bucchero" in this region and by the Greek legends telling of the cruel exploits in that area of the "Tyrrhenian pirates."

But the competition, first of the Phocaeans (battle of Aleria in 545 B.C.), then of the Greeks and later of the Syracusans (battle of Cumae in 474 B.C.), eventually forced the Etruscans to abandon maritime trade. They then concentrated on overland trade, exchanging ceramics and bronze vases with the populations on the other side of the Appennines and, in some cases, even beyond the Alps.

Among the products of the Etruscan economy, some were destined solely for internal consumption, others were sold on local or regional markets and others still, especially during the late republican period and the early imperial age, covered a vast export market. Among the latter, wine was the most important. In fact, in the organization of the villas based on slave labour, the production and export of wine was one of the major sources of revenue for the new large landowners. The export trade was essentially maritime, since overland transport was often impossible and always much more expensive. The wine was carried in ceramic containers, amphoras, and was stored in the holds of large trading ships which sailed from all the major ports and reached the important cities on the western shores of the Mediterranean. The wine then often continued its journey along navigable rivers and was sold even in faraway places. The evidence of this widespread commerce lies in the remains of amphoras discovered by archaeologists. Scholars have studied these amphoras in depth and, among all ceramic objects, they are the best known. But there is still an unanswered question concerning their production: we do not know whether amphoras specifically produced for the export of wine were made by the ceramics industries or by the estates producing the wine. Together with the wine and other foodstuffs, the export trade also dealt with fine tableware produced in various parts of Etruria. In some cases, these objects (Arezzo ceramics, black varnish vases, and so on) have been found in very distant parts of the world. The remarkable commercial success of the produce of Etruria (and of Italy in general) later declined considerably and export was reduced to a regional scale. This was the result of the development of the provinces: Spanish oil, wine from Gaul, African wheat took over and in the end Etruria was even importing fine tableware from the provinces. During the late 1st century A.D. in the countryside around Cosa, the landowners abandoned the wine presses and began to invest in other activities, such as animal breeding. This was the beginning in Etruria, as elsewhere, of the great transformation which brought about the collapse of the manufacturing industries and the spread of the large, underpopulated landed estates.

During the early Middle Ages the main activity in Tuscany, as in the rest of central and northern Italy, was agriculture. Money was used only on exceptional occasions, to buy large quantities of merchandise; normally it was simply hoarded. Most sales and purchases were done by barter. The archaeological evidence from the period of Longobard domination shows us that valuable objects, such as the gold jewellery placed in the tombs with the deceased, were only rarely locally produced, while ceramic wares were almost entirely local. This situation lasted until the 10th century, when Pisa and Genoa challenged the hegemony of Arabs and asserted their supremacy on the coasts and the islands of the Mediterranean. These two cities began to invest their war booty in the construction of mercantile ships which

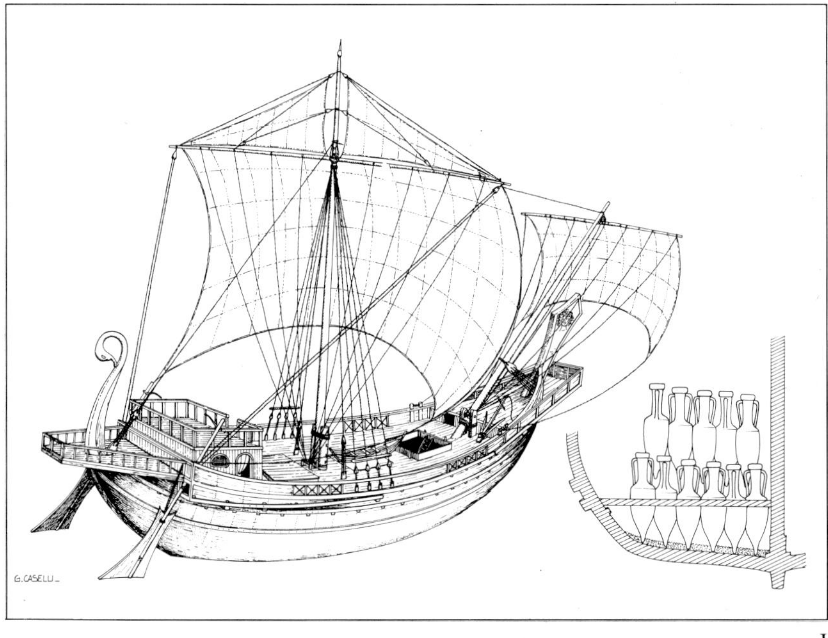

I

carried, as well as the agricultural surplus (mainly oil and wine), also the first Arab ceramics that decorated so many north-western Tuscan churches after the 11th century.

I. Reconstruction of a trade vessel. To the right, cross-section of the hold containing wine amphoras.

II. In the republican period Etruria exported a wide variety of products to the provinces.
Green: Italic pottery
Orange: quality foodstuffs

III. In the imperial age the export of Etruscan products declined, while the importation from the provinces increased.
Yellow: export of local products (wine and pottery)
Blue: wine and fruit
Purple: wine, oil and pottery
Red: wine, oil, fish sauce and pottery
Green: wine and pottery
Brown: wine and pottery
Orange: quality foodstuffs

IV. Amphoras used for transporting wine from Etruria, found in the wreck of a Roman ship near Albenga. Albenga, Civic Museum.

V. Wine amphora with a painted inscription giving the name of the owner (late 7th century B.C.). Vatican, Gregorian Etruscan Museum. During the 7th and 8th centuries Etruscan wine was exported in containers like these to the Western Mediterranean.

VI. Bronze tripod, with sculptural decorations (from Vulci, late 6th century B.C.). Vatican, Gregorian Etruscan Museum. At the top, Hercules and a female figure; at the bottom, three reclining sileni. Similar examples found at Spina, at Dürkheim in Germany and at Athens are evidence of how far-reaching Vulci's export trade was.

VII. Bucchero kantharos (from southern Etruria, late 7th-early 6th century B.C.). Florence, Archaeological Museum. This jug was used for drinking wine; at the height of the Etruscans' maritime expansion, its usage spread throughout the Mediterranean.

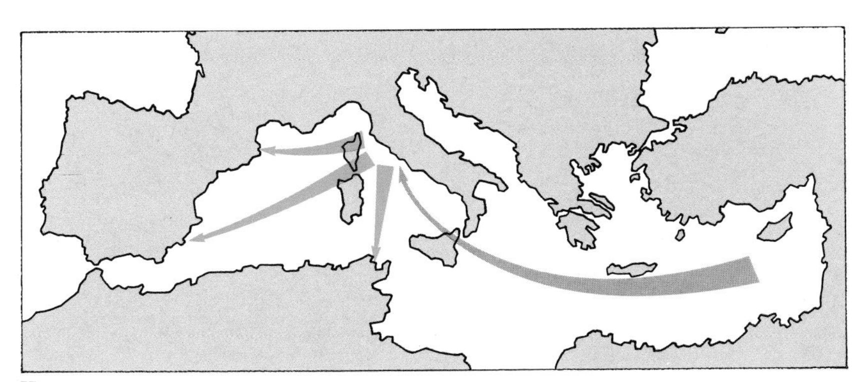
II

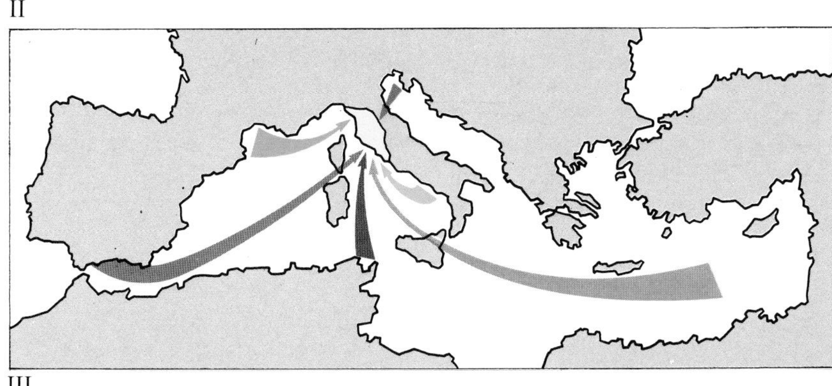
III

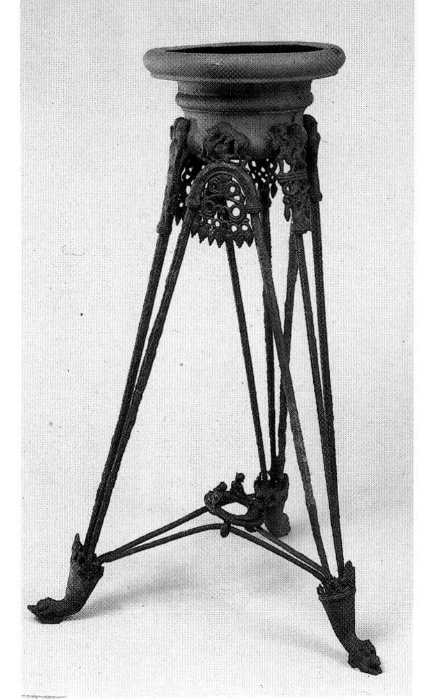
VI

IV

V

VII

131

132

133

131. Cosa, the walls (3rd-2nd century B.C.).

132. Cosa, ruins of the Capitolium (2nd century B.C.).

133. Saturnia, the Clodian Way and the Roman gate (225 B.C.).

allowed them to take over the confiscated land; Rome thus benefited from the traditonally antagonistic relationship between the small towns and the former ruling city.

After the Roman conquest (280 B.C.) VULCI lost the majority of its land which was divided into prefectures and colonies, some founded *ex novo*, others by developing existing communities.

The city probably only kept control over the central-eastern land surrounding it; the coastal stretch, between Vulci and the sea, became public land (*ager publicus*) and the city's port (Regisvilla) was abandoned.

There are ruins and archaeological finds documenting the life of Vulci under the Romans. It was here that Aurelius Cotta's milestone, marking the distance of 70 miles from Rome, was found; Aurelius Cotta was responsible for the construction of the Via Aurelia, probably in 241 B.C. Along the main east-west street of the city (*decumanus*) an inscription documents the restoration of a building during the imperial age. Walking down the *decumanus* one can see the ruins of a late republican house where floor-mosaics with geometrical patterns were found; nearby is an area where the baths stood.

During the 3rd century the prefecture of Statonia (today, Castro) was formed just north of Vulci, and further north, the prefecture of Saturnia. Both these towns, as we have seen, existed before the Roman conquest. On the coast, on the other hand, the Roman colony of COSA (today, Ansedonia) was founded in 273 B.C. The city, whose name probably derived from the earlier Etruscan settlement (located on the site of nearby Orbetello), has been excavated and is today almost entirely open to the public. Surrounded by a polygonal set of walls, like those at Saturnia, Cosa covered an area of over thirty acres; the town-planning was based on the customary straight streets, regularly intersecting at right angles (the *cardines* running north-south, and the *decumani* running east-west). The forum was surrounded by public buildings such as the basilica, the comitium, the curia, and was very similar in plan to the Roman forum. The

134

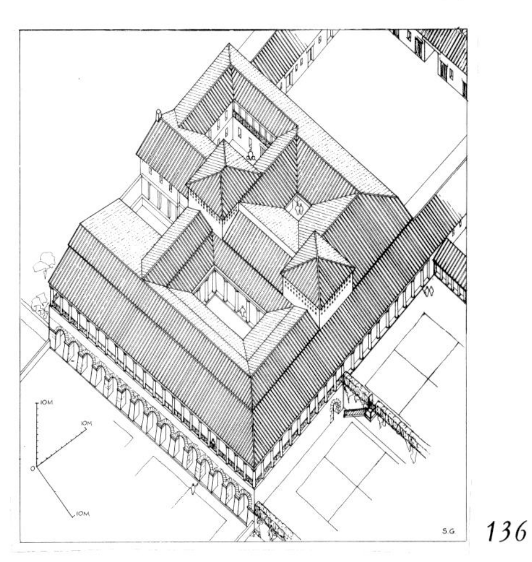

136

135

134. Settefinestre, the fortifications of the Roman villa (1st century B.C.).

135. Settefinestre, the portico of the Roman villa (1st century B.C.).

136. Reconstruction of the villa at Settefinestre.

highest point of the city, the sacred area (*arx*), was where the temples stood. The Capitolium stood on a large platform; it was built in the 2nd century B.C. on the ruins of an older temple dedicated probably to Jupiter. Among the private buildings, a *domus* has been excavated and almost entirely reconstructed near the entrance gate on the south-east side of the city.

137

13

137. Talamone, ruins of the Roman villa at Madonna delle Grazie (1st century A.D.).

138. Talamone, the cistern of the Roman villa at Madonna delle Grazie (1st century A.D.).

There are remains of the walls of SATURNIA, which we mentioned earlier, still visible near the Porta Romana; this was where the Clodian Way, built in 225 B.C. to connect Rome to Saturnia, entered the city. Among the other ruins in Saturnia, a *castellum aquarum* (a public building where the distribution of water took place) has been identified, as well as a group of baths near the present-day sulphur springs.

In the 2nd century Saturnia became a Roman colony (183 B.C.), while the colony of Heba (situated on the site of present-day Magliano) was founded on the coast, north of Cosa, probably between 167 and 157 B.C. Heba was founded on an area of Etruscan territory, presumably allied to Rome, ruled over by the city of TALAMONE. Talamone stood on the hill that today is called Talamonaccio. We know from literary sources that in 225 B.C. the famous battle between the Romans (led by Atilius Regulus and Aemilius Papus) and the Gauls took place on the outskirts of Talamone. The discovery of a mass grave, with remains of men and horses mixed with quicklime, along the coast at Campo Regio is considered to be connected to this battle. Our sources also tell us that Marius landed at Talamone in his search for allies against his enemy Sulla. And it was Sulla who was probably responsible for the sack of the city in 82 B.C. We do not know whether the city managed to survive for any length of time after that; nor do we know whether the numerous small farms that sprang up throughout the countryside are the consequence of the abandoning of the city. What we do know is that Talamone continued to prosper throughout the whole of the 2nd century and this is shown by the new decorations added to the temple on the top of the hill. Among these are several architectural terracottas and the famous pediment (now in the museum in Orbetello) which has recently been dated at the second quarter of the 2nd century B.C. Why such an elaborate new decoration was added at that time is still uncertain. Next to the temple a votive tablet with miniature reproductions of agricultural implements and weapons was found; this has been interpreted as the offering of ex-soldiers (*veterani*) who had been granted land in the new colonies founded nearby (perhaps at the time of the foundation of Heba).

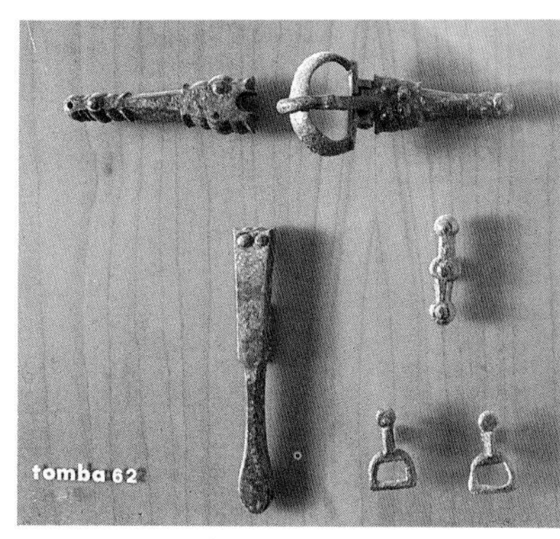

139. *Sovana, the early medieval crypt of the cathedral (7th century).*

140. *Buckle and decorative reliefs from a belt (from Grangia, second half of the 7th century). Grosseto, Archaeological Museum.*

The history of the land along the coast is at present more well known than that of the inland towns. The river Albenga was the boundary between the territory of the colony of Heba, to the north, and Cosa, to the south. As early as the 3rd century B.C. (but the majority of our archaeological evidence dates from the 2nd), the countryside appears to have been dotted with many small farms where the colonizing farmers lived. The excavation of the farm of Giardino Vecchio (near Cosa) has confirmed the theories based on the surface finds: the farms, belonging to peasant smallholders, appear to decline in the early 1st century B.C., at the same time as the development and spread of large estates based on slave labour. The small farms were incorporated into large properties in the hands of wealthy landowners (the presence in the area of the Domitii Oenobardi and the Sixti families is documented).

One of these villas, at SETTEFINESTRE near Cosa, has been completely excavated. The living quarters of the landowners (*pars urbana*) and the agricultural part have been brought to light. The former was elaborately decorated with painted wall plaster, stuccoes and colourful floor mosaics; the other part contained the machinery for the production of wine (exported to almost all the western Mediterranean countries) and oil, the granary, the stables for the animals and the living quarters of the slaves employed in agriculture. This kind of agricultural organization reached its peak between the mid-1st century B.C. and the mid-1st century A.D. and began to decline during the 2nd century. The buildings were abandoned or converted to other uses, and replaced by new, luxurious and enormous constructions, usually along the coast (maritime villas). We have no evidence as yet of any productive activity connected to these new constructions except for the reservoirs for the breeding of fish; but none of them has been systematically excavated. It would be very interesting to establish the connection between the maritime villas and the surrounding countryside, organized as a large landed estate. Among these villas, one should mention the one at Santa Liberata, on the north coast of Monte Argentario, and the one at Madonna delle Grazie, near present-day Talamone. At least a few of these villas, such as the one near Talamone, continued to exist until the late 5th century, surviving the invasion of Alaric and the Goths and despite the fact that the neighbouring inland areas had become progressively more swampy and uninhabitable. Malaria began to spread through the swamps (and continued until quite recently) until the countryside was completely abandoned towards the late imperial age. Rutilius Namatianus, describing his journey from Rome to Gaul betwen 412 and 416, said that the coast of Etruria was deserted.

From this time onwards the total lack of archaeological evidence, which continued throughout the early Middle Ages, coincides with the desertion of the countryside.

From the late imperial age onwards, SOVANA must have ruled over the territories of Cosa (on the coast) and Saturnia (inland). Under the Longobards, it was the seat of a *gastaldo* (chamberlain) and probably exerted supremacy over the other cities of southern Etruria, even though Lucca extended its domains into Sovana's territory where the population must have been very sparse. The rise to power in Sovana of the family of the Aldobrandeschi dates from the 9th century: in 862 Count Ildebrando exchanged with his brother Geremia, Bishop of Lucca, a considerable amount of property he owned in that diocese for those his brother possessed at Sovana and Rusellae. Later, the Aldobrandeschi became a widespread feudal seigneury in southern Tuscany.

The archaeological finds are few but not unimportant. The Longobard presence is documented by objects found in tombs at Sovana: relief plaques and buckles, of a "romance" type, have been found above all in the Maremma area, in particular in the necropolis of Grangia (near Grosseto), dating from the early 7th century. Other contemporary objects, with traditional late-classical relief patterns, have been found at nearby San Martino sul Fiora (late 7th century).

The territory of Sovana, which was still Byzantine in 592, was incorporated into the Longobard state at the time of Agilulf, and for a long time its boundaries were ill-defined. But the objects found at Crocignanello (Pitigliano), and now in the Archaeological Museum in Grosseto, appear to be completely Longobard.

There is very little left of the early medieval buildings in Sovana. The cathedral, dedicated to Saints Peter and Paul, was largely rebuilt in the 14th century, so that there is little left of the 12th-13th century building that, in turn, had replaced the original pre-Romanesque structure. In any case, the octagonal dome can be dated at the 10th century, and the crypt, with a nave and four aisles divided by colonnettes, dates from the 8th. Near the ruins of San Mamiliano, which was probably the first cathedral built on ruins of Etruscan and Roman buildings, there is the Romanesque church of Santa Maria. Here, near the high altar, is a remarkable pre-Romanesque (8th-9th century) ciborium, with four columns with imitation Corinthian capitals and carved ornaments in the shape of leaves, bunches of grapes inside circles, peacocks and doves (see p. 17).

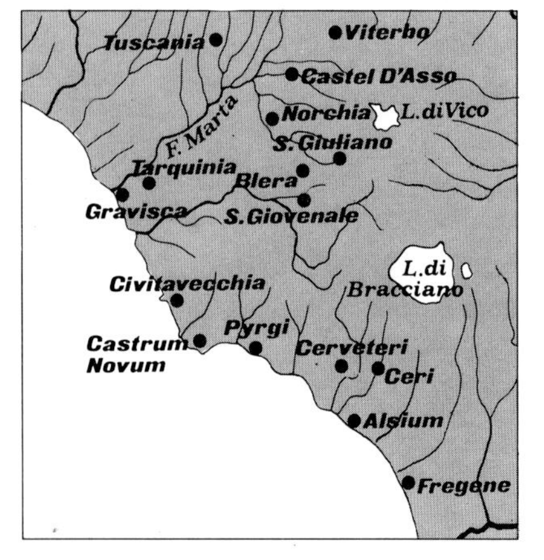

TARQUINIA AND CAERE

The Lower Palaeolithic is well documented at Torre in Pietra and Castel di Guido (where there are also remains of Homo erectus*). The Middle Palaeolithic is present at Castel Malnome and Torre in Pietra; the Upper Palaeolithic at Palidoro and Norchia (Riparo Biedano), and objects in the Pigorini and Villa Giulia Museums. The Neolithic period is documented at Palidoro and at the Patrizi grotto at Sasso di Furbara, where there was a remarkable tomb of a man with a drilled skull (Pigorini Museum). The Aeneolithic is*

141

141. *Tarquinia, Tomb of the Baron (late 6th century B.C.). The frieze shows three scenes of leavetaking: the one on the end wall shows a couple with their two young sons on horseback.*

not well documented: small grotto tombs at Tarquinia, a tomb at Norchia and fragments at Palidoro. The Bronze Age is represented by a variety of finds. Along the coast towards Civitavecchia there are several Appennine culture communities, with dolmen-type graves at Pian Sultano. The largest number of settlements is to be found in the hilly coastal stretch (Appennine, sub-Appennine and proto-Villanovan villages, the latter fortified). At Luni on the Mignone there was an Appennine culture community where Mycenean ceramics of the 14th century B.C. have been found; later objects representing the sub-Appennine and proto-Villanovan cultures were found in the same village. Other settlements, with documentation from the Appennine to the proto-Villanovan, are at San Giovenale and Torrionaccio (Monte Romano). Between Tolfa and Allumiere there are also proto-Villanovan tumulus graves; incineration necropolises are at Allumiere, Costa del Marano (with a rich collection of bronze objects) and at Sasso di Furbara. (Objects at the Pigorini Museum, Villa Giulia Museum, at the Antiquarium of Sasso di Furbara and at the museum of Allumiere).

The pre-eminence of TARQUINIA over all other Etruscan cities is indicated among other things by the legends that attribute its foundation to Tarchon, the friend (or son, or brother) of the mythical Tyrrhenus. And in fact, the Villanovan culture—the earliest Etruscan civilization—found in Tarquinia its highest expression. There were settlements on the two plateaux, called Civita, the side of the future city, and Monterozzi, where huts have been excavated and are now open to the public. The necropolises of Civitucola, Poggio Gallinaro, Poggio Selciatello, Poggio dell'Impiccato, Villa Bruschi, Le Rose and Le Arcatelle were all connected to these settlements (objects now in the museums of Florence and Tarquinia and in the Pigorini Museum). The Tomb of the Warrior, now in Berlin, dates from the late period of this culture; in it a complete armour was

Slavery

I

II

From classical texts and inscriptions we know that in Etruscan society there were various forms of serfdom (total or partial exclusion from civil and political rights), denoted by the lack of a family name. As early as the 6th century B.C. there were slaves who were totally dependent from their masters, and were employed in domestic labour or as craftsmen. An example is the signature of the painter of the Tomb of the Jugglers (late 6th century) in Tarquinia: he signed himself *Aranth Heracanasa*, the first being his individual name, the second the genitive of his master's family name.

Those that Latin writers called *servi* were probably half-free men, that is individuals who were personally free and benefitted from civil rights, such as the right to own property, but had no political rights. This can be deduced from the prophecy of the nymph Vegoia (an Etruscan text of the early 1st century B.C., or according to other scholars of the 3rd century, which has come down to us only in its Latin version) which threatens vengeance on the part of *Tinia*—the Etruscan Jupiter—against all those, masters or serfs, who shall change the borders of their property. The class of the serfs, probably of Italic origin, was responsible from the 4th century onwards for revolts demanding political rights, which in some cases led to Roman intervention . In the 2nd century B.C., in inland northern Etruria where the presence of Rome was less direct, there were slaves whose names were often of Greek origin; they were called *lautni* in Etruscan, derived from the word *lautn* meaning family. During the Hellenistic period, there is evidence of a great number of *lautni* and *servi* being granted freedom; this is documented in particular by old individual names now being used as family names and transmitted from father to son.

In Rome, like in Greece, despite the occasional contrasting opinions, slavery was considered part of the right of the people (*ius gentium*). The slave, *servus*, had no political rights and was not considered a member of the city; he was like an object and, as such, could be bought or sold. Slaves could be bought in slave markets, like the famous one on Delos in the Aegean.

One of the major sources of slaves were wars, since the victor could either kill the enemy or reduce him into slavery and therefore sell him. There were two kinds of slaves: public and private. The former were employed in works of public utility, in manufacturing industries and as craftsmen. They were highly specialized and in some cases became respected professionals. This created deep differences between individual slaves: one might even be the Emperor's private counsellor, while another might spend the rest of his life as a humble stonecutter. The *servi* were sometimes given the permission to have property and ownings, but this permission could be revoked at will by the master. Private slaves were used for domestic labours in the city (*familia urbana*) or for agricultural tasks in the country (*familia rustica*). The ones employed in the countryside were organized in a military fashion: they were divided in groups of ten (*decuriae*), were supervised by *monitores* who were in turn under the control of the *vilicus*. We know from ancient texts that slaves were considered agricultural implements. In fact, the farm's properties were divided into three kinds of instruments: tools (*instrumentum mutum*), animals (*instrumentum semivocale*) and slaves (*instrumentum vocale*). A great deal of care was taken in the upkeep of the slaves, for the death of one of them was considered a great financial loss. They were encouraged to have children, and a female slave who gave birth to four children was granted freedom. When we consider the technology of the classical world, we must point out that these men were in many cases much more efficient than the tools or machineries of the time; in a sense, the slaves were the real Roman technology.

I. Detail of the painted decoration of the Golini I tomb at Orvieto, showing a slave getting wine from a bowl (first half of the 4th century B.C.). Orvieto, Palazzo dei Papi.

II. Relief showing slaves working a winepress. Aquileia, Archaeological Museum.

III. Terracotta urn portraying the hero Echetlo armed only with a plough (from Chiusi, 150-125 B.C.). Rome, Villa Giulia. This kind of urn was often used by slaves, freed men and artisans, as can be seen by the inscriptions; they were made from moulds and produced in large quantities.

IV. Reconstruction of the wine-press in the Roman villa at Settefinestre near Cosa.

III

IV

142

142. Tarquinia, Tomb of Hunting and Fishing (around 530 B.C.). Detail of the end wall showing a fishing scene.

found, as well as bronzes and ceramics in an imitation Cycladic style, proving that Tarquinia was in contact with the first Greek colonizers. After the early "Oriental" stage, represented by the "Bocchoris" tomb (early 7th century) famous for the *fayence* vase with the inscription by the pharaoh of the same name (Tarquinia Museum), the city underwent a period of decline. According to tradition this is when the noble Corinthian merchant Demaratos arrived.

At the beginning of the 6th century a new period of prosperity began for Tarquinia: the harbour temple of GRAVISCA was founded. The inscriptions, in Greek until 480 B.C., show that the temple was dedicated to the worship of Aphrodite, Hera and Demetra; the votive offerings were mostly made by artisans and merchants from eastern Greece. The only exception is the stone anchor-stock dedicated to Apollo around 480 by Sostratos of Aegina, a rich merchant also mentioned by Herodotus. The numerous presence of Greek traders was also responsible for the development, from the first half of the 6th century onwards, of Ionic style artistic productions, such as the stone slabs covering tombs decorated with reliefs (in the local museum) and the earliest painted tombs, dating from after 540. Among these we must mention the tombs of Auguri (Greetings), Giocolieri (Jugglers), Caccia (Hunting), Pesca (Fishing), Tori (Bulls) and Barone (Baron), in some of which the work of immigrant Ionian artists is clearly identifiable.

By the 4th century, Tarquinia controlled a large inland territory

3

144

143. Two terracotta winged horses (from the "Ara della Regina" temple in Tarquinia where they probably were part of the decoration of the main beam; second half of the 4th century B.C.). Tarquinia, National Museum.

144. Cerveteri, Banditaccia necropolis, interior of the Tomb of "Capitelli" (early 6th century B.C.).

(Tuscania, Norchia and Castel d'Asso) developing its agricultural resources and exploiting its position along the communication routes. The powerful ruling family, the *Spurinnas*, owners of the Tomb of the Ogre (Orco), gave Tarquinia the supremacy within the revived Etruscan league, on the eve of the war against Rome (358-351 B.C.). This renewed economic and cultural flourish is revealed also by the reconstruction of the temple called "Ara della Regina" (ruins on the hill of the Civita, while the fictile relief of winged horses is in the museum), by the stone sarcophagi in the museum, some decorated with reliefs, others painted, such as the famous sarcophagus of the Amazons (Archaeological Museum in Florence), and by the painted tombs, showing the new ideology tending towards the glorification of the aristocracy (Orco, Scudi, Giglioli and Tifone tombs). In this last tomb, dating from the late 3rd century B.C., a scene with a procession of magistrates significantly expresses the desire of integration in the Roman state.

The territory of CAERE was densely populated by small settlements in the plains along the coast from the earliest Villanovan period. The objects found in the necropolises around the site of the future city (Sorbo and Cave della Pozzolana) are relatively modest; they can be seen in the local museum and at the Villa Giulia Museum. Even tombs dating from the later Villanovan period have preserved only modest objects, unlike in other parts of Etruria. It is only in the 7th century that the material culture of the city begins to

145

14

145. Hydria from Caere (550-525 B.C.). Rome, Villa Giulia. The decoration shows Hercules leading the three-headed dog Cerberus to King Eurystheus who is frightened and hides in a large jar.

146. Silver cup manufactured in an Oriental workshop, with relief decorations (from the Regolini-Galassi tomb in Caere, 675-650 B.C.). Vatican, Gregorian Etruscan Museum. The outside frieze shows a procession of armed men; the middle one, hunting scenes; the inner roundel, a battle between two lions and a bull.

flourish, thanks probably to the mineral resources of the Tolfa mountains. An aristocratic élite begins to emerge, documented for us by princely tombs of unsurpassed splendour. The Regolini Galassi tomb in the necropolis of Sorbo is the finest example: it consists of a first tumulus (then incorporated into a later one with peripheral tombs) including two long and narrow rooms along the same axis and covered by a false vault. Two niches carved out of the tufa stone open off the first room. The splendid collection of personal objects of the three people buried here is now in the Gregorian Etruscan Museum in the Vatican. It includes very fine gold jewellery, silver cups and chalices, ivory objects, shields, urns, bronze bases, a cart, a throne—some produced locally and some imported from various parts of the Near East—and bucchero and ceramic goods imported from Corinth and eastern Greece. Dating from this same period (second quarter of the 7th century) is the necropolis of Banditaccia, now open to the public, on the plateau to the north-east of the city. Here, an extraordinary quantity of tombs—tumulus, cube-shaped, chamber—illustrates the whole range of funeral architecture in Caere between the 7th and 3rd centuries B.C.

After the 7th century the development of the city caused the population of the territory to concentrate in a few communities (some of which are documented by necropolises open to the public) along the coast (La Scaglia near Civitavecchia, La Castellina near Santa Marinella, Pyrgi, Montetosto, Ceri, Alsium), in the Tolfa mountains, in the valley of the Mignone (Rota, Pisciarelli) and along the border with the territory of Veii (Monterano). Some of them, especially the ones along the borders, were given defence walls in the 4th century. During the 7th and 6th centuries—see the objects in the local museum and at Villa Giulia—as well as the Corinthian, Oriental Greek, Laconian and Attic ceramics imported from Greece, we find artifacts produced locally, principally bucchero. The

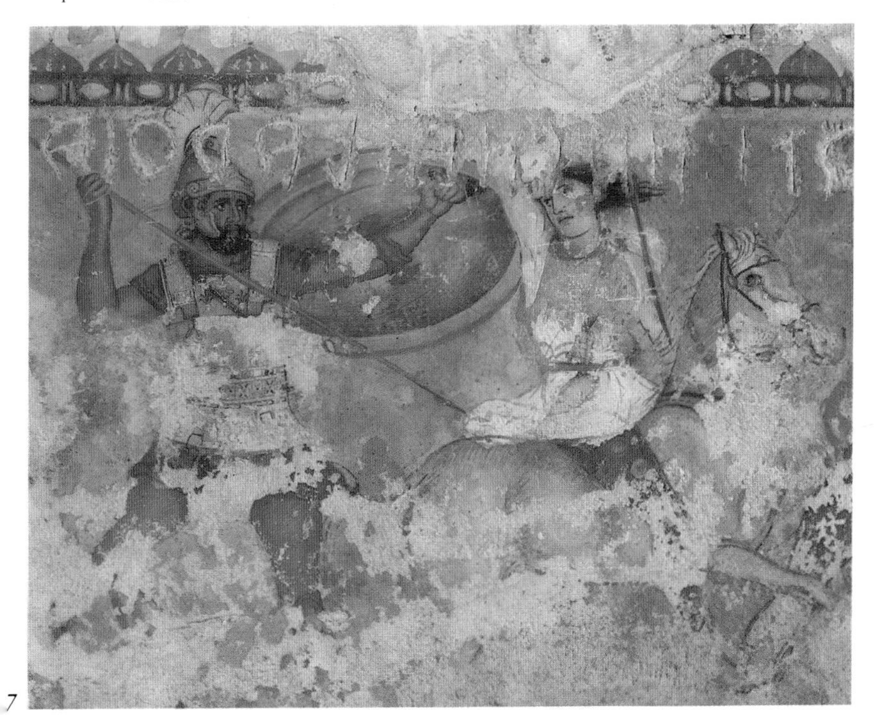

147

148

147. Sarcophagus of the Amazons (from Tarquinia, 350-325 B.C.). Florence, Archaeological Museum. Detail with an Amazon on horseback fighting a Greek warrior; on the outside there is an inscription recording that the sarcophagus is dedicated to Ramtha Hucznai by her son.

148. San Giovenale, excavations of houses. The ground-plan of the town dates from the 6th-5th century B.C.

invention of bucchero was the work of the craftsmen of Caere, as is shown by tomb No. 2 at Casaletti di Ceri in the local museum, by the Calabresi tomb in the Gregorian Museum and by the Montetosto tumulus at Villa Giulia. Etruscan-Corinthian ceramics, such as the large amphoras, the coloured group of bizzarre figures or the "human mask group," exported to southern France, were found in later tombs. And finally, dating from the mid-6th century, there are the "hydrias from Caere," the work of an immigrant Aeolian artist who painted scenes from Greek mythology, especially the labours of Hercules, in a lighthearted and playful spirit. During this period the development of a sort of "middle class" composed of pro-Greek merchants and craftsmen (see the *Thesauros* at Delphi) is documented by the new tombs in the north-eastern part of the Banditaccia necropolis: these are no longer tumuli, but die-shaped tombs, and they are placed next to each other in straight lines, indicating that the deceased were all considered equals. Also in the second half of the 6th century, when the city allied with the Carthaginians against the naval power of the Phocaean Greeks (battle of Aleria, 545 B.C.), a large number of public buildings were constructed: the temples at Montetosto and Furbara, the temple of Vigna Zoccoli (in the city) with inscriptions in Greek to the goddess Hera (in the local museum). The sacred area in the port of PYRGI was enlarged and enriched by *Thefarie Velianas*, who is referred to as king of Caere in a gold foil with a Phoenician inscription, but was probably a tyrannical figure supported by the plebeians. The sanctuary was connected to the city by a monumental gate: it consisted of a Greek type temple (B) dedicated to the Etruscan goddess *Uni* (the same as the Latin Juno and the Greek Hera) and the Punic goddess Astarte, and a later Etruscan type temple (A). The excavations and the Antiquarium are open to the public; the fictile high-relief from temple A showing the battle between Tidaeus and Melanippus and copies of the three gold

149

150

149. Stone relief showing the battle between Tydeus and Melanippus, with Athena and Zeus looking on (from Temple A at Pyrgi, around 460 B.C.). Rome, Villa Giulia.

150. Pyrgi, excavations on the site of Temple B (late 6th century B.C.).

foil inscriptions (two in Etruscan, one in Punic) commemorating the dedication of the temple are in the Villa Giulia Museum. A school of ceramic workers, working at first in the Ionic style and later in the Aeginan, was active at this time, producing among other things the architectural sculptures from Pyrgi and the Sarcophagus "degli Sposi" in Villa Giulia, and a sarcophagus lid with a young man at a banquet (Cerveteri museum).

After a period of cultural isolation (second half of the 5th century), characterized only by the importations from Attica found in the "Tomb of the Greek Vases" (Villa Giulia) and by the foundation, towards the end of the century, of the "Tomb of the Sarcophagi" (local museum and Gregorian Museum), the city experienced a cultural revival. The sanctuary at Pyrgi was restored after it had been sacked by Dionysius of Syracuse (384 B.C.) and new tombs were founded, such as the "Tomb of the Reliefs," decorated with painted stuccoes showing weapons and utensils of daily usage. During the invasion of the Gauls in 390, the Roman vestal virgins took refuge in Caere, for, unlike its traditional enemy Veii, the city was allied to Rome and was soon granted the rights of Roman citizenship excluding the vote (*civitas sine suffragio*). This alliance explains the presence in Caere of several important Roman citizens, documented by the tomb of the Claudii (who changed their name to the more Etruscan *Clavtie*) and by inscriptions in Latin and Etruscan on "Genucilia" disks, a typical local product. The good relations between Caere and Rome continued throughout the 4th century (with the only exception of the war between Rome and Tarquinia in 358-351), until the early 3rd century when Caere joined the other cities of southern Etruria in their revolt against Rome.

The territory between Ferento-Acquarossa to the north and San Giovenale to the south, comprising the basin of the Fosso Biedano and the upper valley of the Mignone, has all the characteristics of a communication route, beginning from the archaic period until the late 3rd or early 2nd century B.C. when the Clodian Way was built. This area was the land of Caere and Tarquinia and the material culture was influenced by these two towns, predominantly by Caere in the archaic period, and by Tarquinia from the 4th century B.C. on-

Hilltop Towns in Tuscany: Scarlino

Fortified hilltop villages are one of the fundamental aspects of medieval and modern Tuscany. The development of these settlements can be studied primarily thanks to archaeology, for it is not until the 11th century that written documentation begins to be at all abundant. Some recent excavations have shown us how complex the phenomenon really is and how many transformations these settlements have undergone. The case of Scarlino is exemplary. It was a castle documented from the end of the 1th century, on the border between the dioceses of Roselle on one side and Populonia and Massa on the other. The early medieval settlement, consisting in huts with fireplaces and a frescoed church, grew up on a site of much earlier communities. There are, in fact, traces of a late Bronze Age settlement (12th-11th century B.C.) which was then practically abandoned during the archaic Etruscan period; between the 5th and 1st centuries B.C. there was a large hilltop fortress, surrounded by walls that were more than two metres thick. During the imperial age, the site was all but abandoned, while the area at the foot of the hill and along the coast became populated by villas and other smaller farming communities. When the early medieval settlement developed it followed a model that was more than a thousand years old. The hilltop had probably been fortified since it was first settled, but during the 10th century the fortifications had to be strengthened. Even the houses became more solid and the huts were replaced by stone houses with terracotta roof tiles, surrounded by a huge set of walls that enclosed the whole hilltop. The village underwent several renovations until the 13th century: for example, the old church was replaced by a new Romanesque one. But, basically, its general appearance did not change much. It was only at the beginning of the 14th century that serious changes took place. The area occupied by the original castle was taken over by a fort and a new set of walls was built around the houses that had grown up outside the original settlement, including the Romanesque church of San Donato, built in the first half of the 13th century.

I. Ground-plan of the castle of Scarlino.

II. The castle of Scarlino.

III. Scarlino. The interior of the citadel: early medieval beam holes, Hellenistic and medieval elements.

IV. Scarlino. Inside the 15th-century church there are the ruins of the apses of two churches: above, the Romanesque one and at the centre, the 9th-century one.

II

III

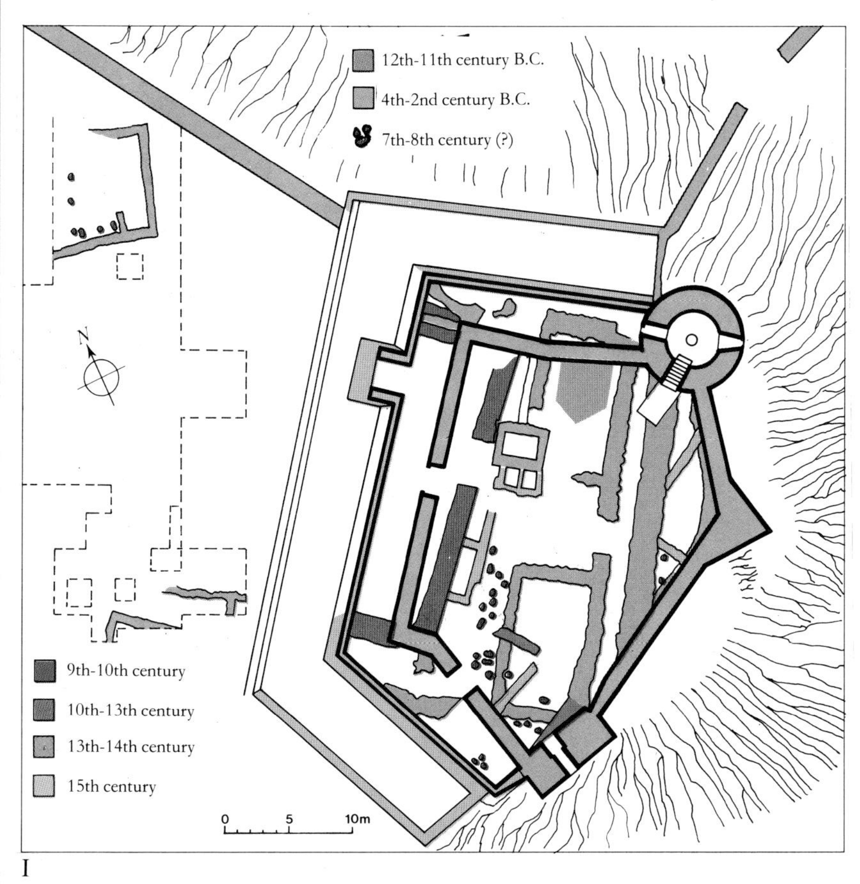

I

IV

151

153

152

151. Castel D'Asso, facade of tomb 53, with a fake door and the inscription above it giving the name of the owner, Arnthal Ceises (6th century B.C.).

152. Norchia, the hillside necropolis (4th-3rd century B.C.).

153. Stone sarcophagus showing a reclining couple (from Caere, late 6th century B.C.). Rome, Villa Giulia.

wards. Three of the very few excavations of private houses in Etruria are in this region: ACQUAROSSA, with private houses and an aristocratic residence built around a square internal courtyard with porticoes, and LUNI and SAN GIOVENALE in the upper valley of the Mignone. Another characteristic of this area are the spectacular mountain necropolises carved out of the rock: BLERA and SAN GIULIANO, used in archaic times, CASTEL D'ASSO and NORCHIA, dating from the later period.

The long struggle against Rome was finally concluded with TARQUINIA's defeat in 281 B.C. The city was forced to surrender a large stretch of coastland which became public land (*ager publicus*) and its control over the towns and villages of its territory, which rapidly began to acquire a greater degree of autonomy.

During the 2nd century B.C. Tarquinia's old port, which had been abandoned after the defeat, resumed activity thanks to the foundation of the Roman colony of Gravisca in 181 B.C.. The plan of this town, like most other coastal colonies, is similar to that of a military camp (*castrum*) with streets running parallel to each other. At the end of the civil war (90 B.C.), the towns in the area which had already become independent of Tarquinia became *municipia*.

During the Augustan period, despite all attempts at increasing the population (as at Gravisca), a period of irreversible decline began for Tarquinia and it continued all through the imperial age.

Roman presence at Tarquinia is documented, among other things, by a street near the *Ara Reginae*, a sacred building restored many times, even during the imperial age. Also in the centre of Tarquinia are the ruins of a small house, with a large pilastered room next to it: here there were *dolia* for the preservation of foodstuffs. Roman control over the area caused the extinction of some large local families and the entry of others into the Roman senate. The latter were responsible for the construction of many public buildings. In the early imperial age the *elogia* of the *Spurinnae* (an important local family whose members were *aruspices* in Rome and even became consuls) were placed in the *Ara Reginae* together with the statue of Tarchon, the mythical founder of Tarquinia, and the *fasti* of the col-

154

155

154. Sarcophagus of the Magistrate (from Caere, Tomb of the Sarcophagi, late 5th century B.C.). Vatican, Gregorian Etruscan Museum. The frieze shows the journey to Hades of the deceased on a chariot, with a procession including three musicians and a man carrying a staff.

155. Blera, a tomb in the necropolis (6th century B.C.).

lege of sixty *haruspices*, who interpreted for the Roman senate the meaning of unusual or exceptional events. The decline, which began in the 3rd century, is documented by the scarsity of archaeological finds, with the exception of a very grand late classical house in the centre of Gravisca.

Defeated by the Romans in the 273 B.C., CAERE lost about half of its territory, in particular the coastal area; many towns that until that time had served primarily as centres of worship (e.g. Pyrgi) were abandoned. Some coastal colonies are founded in the region: from south to north, Fregenae which became a colony in 245 B.C., Alsium, near a previous Etruscan settlement, founded in 247 B.C., and Pyrgi, founded in 264 B.C. on the site of the most important port on Caere's territory before the Roman conquest.

The colony of PYRGI is surrounded by a set of polygonal walls, similar to those of Cosa, founded in the same period. The harbour, which is today underwater, has been identified by aerial photographs. The colony of CASTRUM NOVUM (near present-day Santa Marinella) was also founded in 264 B.C. near an earlier settlement. We know from an inscription that the town had a theatre, a *curia* (the seat of the colony's magistrates) and a *tabularium* (the town's archive). All these newly founded coastal towns had the function of controlling both the sea and the Etruscan inland, still not completely subjugated. The construction of the Via Aurelia (probably in 241 B.C.) connected these centres to one another and to the other towns along the coast as far as Cosa.

The inland territory was organized as a prefecture under the rule of a magistrate nominated directly by Rome (*praefectus*). No new colonies were founded in this area, unlike what happened along the coast, and the only new town that was built was Forum Clodii, founded in the 2nd century along the Clodian Way (built in 225 B.C.) connecting Rome to Saturnia.

During the republican age many villas were built, both along the coast and in the inland. We do not know whether the maritime villas (which became more numerous and important in the early and middle imperial age) were the centres of productive activities like the ones in the inland, but we do know that they had large pools

156

159

157

160

158

156. Tarquinia, the paving of the port.

157. Santa Marinella, ruins of the late republican period villa at Grottacce.

158. Gravisca, a dolium used for the preservation of food, from a late republican period private house.

159. Santa Marinella, ruins of the Roman villa at Grottacce.

160. Pyrgi, the Castrum (3rd century B.C.).

used for fish-breeding. Near ALSIUM (between San Nicola and Palo) there were several villas—one of which belonged to Pompey. The most interesting are the one at the castle of Palo, with polychrome mosaics now in the castle itself, and the one at San Nicola. Among the villas around Castrum Novum, we must mention the one at Grottacce, with very large fishponds.

During the Augustan age the area experienced a new period of prosperity. At Caere, a theatre, a *caesareum* (where the Caesars were honoured) and other important public buildings, such as an aqueduct, were built. Nothing remains of these constructions today. It seems that during this period Caere was once again granted the status of autonomous *municipium*, but it was probably only a formality, for in practice the city's subordination to Rome continued unchanged.

Despite Augustus's attempts at reviving the cities of this area, they continued to decline. During the imperial age this decadence became even more pronounced and by the 2nd century A.D. all the more important cities were abandoned. The villas appear to have remained the only active elements in a territory which was becoming

161

162

161. Tuscania, the hill of San Pietro with the apses of the churches of Santa Maria Maggiore and San Pietro.

162. Tuscania, San Giusto, the crypt consisting of three cellae trichorae *with a cross-vault resting on columns taken from a ruined classical building. This is the oldest architectural structure in Tuscania.*

progressively more the property of the emperor.

It was Trajan who was responsible for the last important intervention in the region (107-108 A.D.): the construction of the harbour of Centumcellae (Civitavecchia). This port and the surrounding town are the only ones that survived until the 5th century, as we know from Rutilius Namatianus. Travelling through the area at the beginning of the 5th century, he was struck by Centumcellae's vitality compared to the rest of the coastland, which was already an uninhabited marshland.

East of the city, on a hill overlooking the harbour, there are the remains of Trajan's famous villa (mistakenly identified with the site of Aquae Tauri). It consists of a smaller nucleus, built during the late republican period, and a larger one, built later. Among the ruins, scholars have identified several large rooms used as baths, a library and the *hospitalia* (apartments for guests). Fragments of the villas floor decorations are now in the museum at Civitavecchia. The site of Aquae Tauri is present-day Ficoncella, near a sulphur spring.

TUSCANIA, which became the seat of a diocese only in 649, played an important role under the Longobards as a border town, in the centre of a territory with several pre-existing *civitas* (Tarquinia, Ferentis, as well as the future Viterbo, a newly founded town not far from the abandoned *civitas* of the Sorrinenses). In the early Middle Ages the development of Tuscania is connected to its position along the Clodian Way, between the Cassian and the Aurelian, on a fairly flat stretch of land connected to the sea by the river Marta, navigable at the time. On the hill of San Pietro the Romanesque church of the same name is interesting for the presence of early medieval motifs in its decoration. Here, recent excavations have brought to light archaeological strata from the late Bronze Age to the Modern Era. The early medieval levels document the existence of buildings probably made out of wood. But the most important early medieval find is not quite in the centre of the town: it is the crypt of San Giusto, consisting of three *cellae trichorae*, with cross-vaults without intrados and barrel-vaults. The architectural design is reminiscent of the crypt of San Salvatore on Mount Amiata and also has similarities with the crypt of the abbey of Farneta in the Chiana valley.

Museums of Etruria

ALBANO LAZIALE – CIVIC MUSEUM
The archaeological section houses local materials from the prehistorical, proto-historical, Roman and early Christian periods.

ALLUMIERE – PREHISTORICAL MUSEUM OF UPPER LATIUM
Materials from prehistorical and proto-historical periods, including Villanovan vases and objects from Etruscan tombs.

AREZZO
MECENATE ÅRCHAEOLOGICAL MUSEUM
Prehistorical materials and Etruscan and Roman urns, ceramics, bronzes and statues. The collection of the so-called 'vasi Aretini' is particularly interesting.

ASCIANO – ETRUSCAN MUSEUM
Objects from the necropolises of Poggio Pinci.

BOLOGNA – CIVIC ARCHAEOLOGICAL MUSEUM
A vast collection of prehistorical, Villanovan, Etruscan, Roman and medieval materials from the region around Bologna and also from other parts of Italy. Particularly interesting are the furniture items and household implements.

CAPENA – ANTIQUARIUM OF LUCUS FERONIAE
Objects from the excavation of Lucus Feroniae and the necropolis of Capena.

CASOLA IN LUNIGIANA
ARCHAEOLOGICAL MUSEUM
Prehistorical materials and stele-statues from Lunigiana.

CECINA – CIVIC ANTIQUARIUM
Materials from local excavations, in particular from an Etruscan tomb and a Roman villa.

CERVETERI – NATIONAL MUSEUM
Villanovan, Etruscan and Roman materials from the area around Cerveteri: vases, sarcophagi, terracottas and funerary objects.

CHIUSI – NATIONAL ETRUSCAN MUSEUM
A vast collection of Etruscan and Roman materials from excavations in the area: ceramics, cinerary urns, sarcophagi and bronzes.

CIVITA CASTELLANA
NATIONAL FALISCAN MUSEUM
Archaeological finds dating from the 10th to the 3rd centuries B.C. found in the Faliscan Plain.

CIVITAVECCHIA
NATIONAL ARCHAEOLOGICAL MUSEUM
Villanovan, Etruscan, Roman and medieval materials from excavations in the area.

COLLE VAL D'ELSA
ARCHAEOLOGICAL MUSEUM
Etruscan funerary objects, ceramics and coins from local excavations or acquired as gifts.

CORTONA – MUSEUM OF THE ETRUSCAN ACADEMY
Etruscan and Roman gold jewellery, coins, ceramics and bronzes from various sites.

FIESOLE – ARCHAEOLOGICAL MUSEUM
Materials from the excavations of the nearby Etruscan temple and from the Roman theatre and baths.

FLORENCE – ARCHAEOLOGICAL MUSEUM OF CENTRAL ETRURIA
Prehistorical materials from excavations in Tuscany. Etruscan and Roman sculptures, bronzes, urns, ceramics, gold jewellery and coins which formed the Medici and Lorraine collections, originally housed in the Uffizi. Etruscan monuments and tombs have been reconstructed in the topographical section.

FLORENCE
FLORENTINE PREHISTORICAL MUSEUM
Prehistorical objects (weapons, implements, graffiti) and didactic material illustrating the various prehistorical cultures.

GROSSETO – ARCHAEOLOGICAL MUSEUM
Prehistorical materials, Etruscan and Roman funerary objects, urns, statues, bronzes and coins from the local excavations, in particular at Rusellae. Also a small section of medieval archaeology.

GROTTAFERRATA
MUSEUM OF THE ABBEY OF SAN NILO
Prehistorical and Etruscan materials.

GUBBIO – CIVIC MUSEUM
Inscriptions, statues, coins and other objects from the proto-historical and Roman periods, from the Roman theatre and local excavations.

ISCHIA DI CASTRO – CIVIC ANTIQUARIUM
Materials from the excavations of the Etruscan necropolises of Castro.

LA SPEZIA – CIVIC MUSEUM
Prehistorical, proto-historical, Roman and early Christian materials from the excavations at Luni. The collection of stele-statues is particularly interesting.

LUCCA – NATIONAL MUSEUM AT VILLA GUINIGI
Etruscan and Roman materials as well as an important medieval section including objects from excavations in the area around Lucca.

LUNI – NATIONAL ARCHAEOLOGICAL MUSEUM
Materials from the excavations at Luni, primarily dating from the Roman period.

MARCIANA – ARCHAEOLOGICAL MUSEUM
Prehistorical and Roman materials from various communities on the island of Elba.

MASSA – CASTELLO MALASPINA
Permanent exhibition of prehistorical and Roman materials from the area.

MASSA MARITTIMA
ARCHAEOLOGICAL MUSEUM
Objects from the Etruscan tombs of the area and a collection of Roman coins.

MONTALCINO – ARCHAEOLOGICAL MUSEUM
Prehistorical and Etruscan materials from the area.

ORBETELLO – CIVIC ANTIQUARIUM
Etruscan and Roman funerary objects and other materials from the excavations in the area, in particular from Cosa.

ORTONOVO
NATIONAL ARCHAEOLOGICAL MUSEUM
Roman archaeological finds from the excavations in the area around Luni.

ORVIETO – FAINA MUSEUM
Archaeological finds mostly from the Etruscan necropolises around Orvieto. The collection of Greek and Etruscan vases is particularly interesting.

ORVIETO – CATHEDRAL MUSEUM
The archaeological section houses funerary objects from the necropolises around Orvieto.

PERUGIA – NATIONAL ARCHAEOLOGICAL MUSEUM OF UMBRIA
Prehistorical materials from central Italy. Urns, bronze laminae and funerary objects from the Etruscan necropolises of the area. Bas-reliefs and inscriptions from the Roman period.

PISA – MUSEO DELL'OPERA DELLA PRIMAZIALE
An archaeological collection of Etruscan and Roman statues, sarcophagi and architectural fragments.

PONTREMOLI
CIVIC ARCHAEOLOGICAL MUSEUM
Prehistorical and Roman finds from Lunigiana, in particular stele-statues.

POPULONIA – ETRUSCAN MUSEUM
Vases, fragments of sarcophagi and funerary obiects from the excavations of the Etruscan necropolises of Populonia.

ROME – CAPITOLINE MUSEUMS
Etruscan vases and funerary objects. Sculptures, mosaics, coins and other materials from excavations of Roman sites.

ROME – MUSEUM OF THE INSTITUTE OF ETRUSCAN STUDIES
Casts and reconstructions of Etruscan cities and settlements.

ROME – PIGORINI PREHISTORICAL AND ETHNOGRAPHICAL MUSEUM
Materials from the palaeolithic, aeneolithic, bronze and iron ages, from all over Italy and in particular from Latium.

ROME – NATIONAL ETRUSCAN MUSEUM AT VILLA GIULIA
Proto-historical, Italic and Etruscan materials from Latium, southern Etruria and Umbria. Sculptures, ceramics, bronzes, gold jewellery, funerary objects and other materials from excavations, arranged topographically.

ROME, VATICAN
GREGORIAN ETRUSCAN MUSEUM
Sculptures, ceramics, bronzes, gold jewellery, funerary objects and other materials from excavations in the necropolises of southern Etruria. The objects from the Regolini-Galassi tomb at Cerveteri are particularly interesting.

SAN GIMIGNANO – ETRUSCAN MUSEUM
Etruscan archaeological finds from various excavations in the area.

SATURNIA – ANTIQUARIUM
Etruscan and Roman materials form excavations in the area.

SIENA – NATIONAL ARCHAEOLOGICAL MUSEUM
Prehistorical materials, Etruscan and Roman urns, sarcophagi, sculptures and ceramics from excavations around Siena (Val d'Elsa, Amiata, Chiusi).

SPOLETO – ARCHAEOLOGICAL MUSEUM
Prehistorical objects, Roman and medieval sculptures, inscriptions and architectural fragments.

TARQUINIA – NATIONAL ETRUSCAN MUSEUM
Etruscan materials from the necropolises of the area: sarcophagi, detached frescoes, vases, bas-reliefs and funerary objects.

TERNI – ARCHAEOLOGICAL MUSEUM
Proto-historical materials from the necropolises of the area.

TERNI – ARCHAEOLOGICAL COLLECTION AT PALAZZO CARRARA
Sarcophagi, inscriptions, steles and other Roman and medieval materials.

TODI – ETRUSCAN ROMAN MUSEUM
Italic, Etruscan and Roman sculpture, gold jewellery, ceramics and inscriptions.

TUSCANIA – NATIONAL MUSEUM
Materials from excavations in Tuscania and the surrounding area; in particular sarcophagi.

VETULONIA – CIVIC ARCHAEOLOGICAL MUSEUM
Materials from excavations in the city: funerary objects and Villanovan, Etruscan and Roman ceramics.

VITERBO – CIVIC MUSEUM
Villanovan, Etruscan and Roman materials from excavations in the area around Viterbo.

VOLTERRA – GUARNACCI ETRUSCAN MUSEUM
Prehistorical materials; a wide range of Etruscan cinerary urns, Etruscan and Roman gold jewellery, sculpture, ceramics, coins and other materials from the area around Volterra.

VULCI – NATIONAL MUSEUM
Villanovan, Etruscan and Roman archaeological finds from the area.

Index of Places